Primitive Methodism

Exploring Methodism

Primitive Methodism

Geoffrey Milburn

EPWORTH PRESS

Copyright © Geoffrey Milburn 2002

British Library Cataloguing in Publication data

A catalogue record for this book is available
from the British Library

0 7162 05548

First published in 2002
by Epworth Press
20 Ivatt Way
Peterborough PE3 7PG

Typeset by Rowland Phototypesetting Limited,
Bury St Edmunds, Suffolk
and printed in Great Britain by
Biddles Ltd

Contents

Preface and Acknowledgements

Writing this book has roused in me a strong sense of indebtedness which has very deep roots, reaching back into childhood days. These earliest thoughts and images gather round the former Primitive Methodist Chapel at Hutton Rudby, near Stokesley, in North Yorkshire, where most of the extended family of which I was one of the youngest members gathered for worship and fellowship. At the time it seemed to me that the entire congregation consisted of relatives of ours and, if they were not, they behaved as if they were!

Certain ministers virtually fell into this same category. For instance, long after their terms of service in the Stokesley Circuit, John Upright and Albert Bell happened to be stationed in places where the chances of army service and university education had led my own steps. And as a matter of form I was invited to partake of their hospitality. I knew virtually nothing of the history of Primitive Methodism in those distant days but I had learned something of its character as an extended family.

It was many years later that I became fascinated by the history of Primitive Methodism as an academic interest. Once again it was in large part a result of kindness on the part of folk who seemed moved to hand over to me copies of Primitive Methodist books and magazines. Eventually a whole bedroom had to be allocated to them and the collection is still growing! The result was that I began to undertake serious research into the Primitive Methodist Connexion, to give talks about it, and write monographs on aspects of its history. In the process contacts with other like-minded folk were developing, ideas exchanged, mutual services rendered and friendships forged.

For the help I received in this process of learning I owe many debts, of which a few only can be acknowledged here. To the late John Duncan, who spontaneously handed over to me a considerable library of books which laid the foundation of my Primitive Methodist collection, and the late Miss Dorothy Butterfield of Sunderland, for the same kindness. To Stephen Hatcher for helpfulness with regard to Primitive Methodist books and magazines, and for his own researches and his initiatives in the promotion of the Englesea Brook Chapel and Museum. To the late William Leary for friendship and interest and especially for his invaluable *Directory of Primitive Methodist Ministers and Their Circuits*,

1990; to the staff of the Methodist Chapel Aid office in York for practical help and kindness; to friends and colleagues in the Wesley Historical Society, in particular John Vickers, Colin Dews, Margaret Batty, Dorothy Graham and Alan Rose; and, finally, to my wife Mary who has been an ever-helpful, adept and patient secretary, and much else besides.

Geoffrey E. Milburn

Introduction

The adjective 'Primitive' has long been a cause of misunderstanding with regard to the reputation of the branch of Methodism which bore that name. It has conjured up in many minds a picture of a crude and unsophisticated movement, both in its character and its members, an image reinforced by the Primitive Methodists' alternative name of 'Ranters'. It is likely that this latter term was applied to the Primitive Methodists in response to their loud and impassioned open-air preaching, praying and singing. Nevertheless it may have been suggested also by a confused folk memory of the seventeenth-century Ranters, a sect whose persuasions John Bunyan was tempted by but staunchly resisted because of their antinomian beliefs. The name Ranters was first applied to the Primitive Methodists at Belper in Derbyshire in 1816, and soon fell into such common use that the Connexion was obliged, if somewhat reluctantly, to accept it and even use it in some of its published literature in the early years.

The Primitive Methodists' true name, however, was quite deliberately accepted by the early founders and had a clear purpose and meaning. This was not invented by them, but was a phrase in fairly common use in the later years of the eighteenth century to refer to the Methodism of Wesley's early period. John Hampson, in his *Memoirs of John Wesley* (1791), used the phrase 'primitive Methodists' to make a slighting comment on the 'wild-fire' preachers of early Methodism.[1] More significantly, John Wesley in his later years spoke of 'primitive Methodism' in a more positive sense, as he looked back with nostalgia to the pioneering enthusiasm and simplicity of his movement in its early period and compared it with the more staid institution it was becoming in the later decades of the eighteenth century. A pamphlet published by him entitled *Sufferings of the Primitive Methodists at Wednesbury* (relating to events which occurred in 1743) was still being offered for sale in 1792.

The adoption of Primitive Methodism as the name of the new movement led by Hugh Bourne and William Clowes was therefore a clear declaration that its intended character and purpose was to renew the mission for the conversion of England begun by Wesley seven decades earlier and, as far as possible, to employ the evangelical strategy and methods of Wesley's earlier period, adapted to changing times and circumstances. The significant entry in Hugh Bourne's *Journal* recording this decision is as follows [1]:

1. 'Thursday February 13th, 1812, We called a meeting and made plans for the next quarter, and made some other regulations: in particular we took the name of THE SOCIETY OF THE PRIMITIVE METHODISTS.' The guiding hand in this development was probably not that of Hugh Bourne, who frankly admitted later that he had become drowsy towards the end of the meeting when the decision about the name was taken. There is a tradition that the principal advocate of the name Primitive Methodists was James Crawfoot, the so-called 'mystic of Delamere Forest', and leader of the 'Magic Methodists'. The story may well be true and is worth recording in the words of W. E. Farndale:

> In 1790 John Wesley visited the city of Chester. He thus addressed the Methodist preachers: 'Fellow labourers, wherever there is an open door, enter in and preach the Gospel. If it be to two or three under a hedge or a tree, preach the Gospel. Go out quickly into the streets and lanes of the city and bring in the poor, the maimed, the halt, and the blind. And after you have done this, you will have to say like the servant in the Gospel: Lord, it is done as thou hast commanded, and yet there is room!' Then lifting up his slender hands, while the tears flowed down his venerable face, he exclaimed: 'and yet there is room!' He then added with emphasis: 'And this was the way the primitive Methodists did.' Wesley died the next year and this injunction of his carried, in retrospect, all the force of a last parting word from the founder of Methodism. James Crawfoot was present at that Chester gathering and Wesley's moving exhortation made an indelible impression upon him. Now a score of years later it seemed to come as a personal directive from Wesley himself. For on 13 February 1812, in a meeting at Tunstall, the question arose what was to be the designation of the new body that had come into being. Various titles were proposed and each in turn rejected. Then James Crawfoot rose and cited John Wesley's speech at Chester. That at once settled it.

Source: Hugh Bourne, *Journal*, quoted by William Edward Farndale, *The Secret of Mow Cop*, Wesley Historical Society Lectures, no. 16, London: Epworth Press, 1950, pp. 43–4. See also John Thomas Wilkinson, *Hugh Bourne 1772–1852*, London: Epworth Press, 1952, pp. 77–85, 92 and note.

There is a yet deeper meaning associated with the adjective 'Primitive'. In their work of evangelizing and church building both John and Charles Wesley, and Hugh Bourne and William Clowes, were keenly aware of the model provided by the truly Primitive Christianity of the Apostolic age. In 1748 Wesley observed that in the shaping of Methodism he and his followers had been largely guided by common sense and scripture, and adds that 'they generally found, in looking back, something in Christian Antiquity likewise, very nearly parallel thereto'.[2] Half a century later Hugh Bourne, who had a formidable knowledge of Church history from its beginnings, sensed a rediscovery of early Christianity in the renewal movement out of which, as a result of practical wisdom and good leadership, Primitive Methodism was to take shape.

For the sake of clarification it may be useful here to mention an Irish

Methodist secession of 1816 which took the name of the Primitive Wesleyans. Their title was chosen because they sought to be faithful to Wesley's insistence that Methodism should retain its links with the Church of England and that Methodists should receive the sacrament of Holy Communion only from the hands of an episcopally ordained clergyman. These Primitive Wesleyans reunited with their parent body in 1878.[3]

Thomas Percival Bunting, in his biography of his father Jabez Bunting, while commenting kindly on the Primitive Methodists ('a body of whom it is a real pleasure to speak well') concludes that their choice of name 'savours of injustice to the mother Church', namely, the Wesleyan Connexion. He is implying that the Primitive Methodists in assuming their name claimed to be more truly representative of John Wesley (at least in his evangelical prime) than the Wesleyans themselves. He refers also to the Primitive Wesleyans as making a similar claim with regard to Wesley's Anglican convictions and loyalties, which the Wesleyan Connexion was being forced to adjust as it increasingly took the shape of an independent church. T. P. Bunting found some comfort in the fact that these two very different secessions (sacramentalist on the one hand and evangelical on the other) both took the name Primitive and concluded that 'probably neither was right'![4]

I

Origins

The period of English history in which Primitive Methodism appeared was tumultuous by any reckoning. Europe had been shaken by the impact of the French Revolution and the ensuing wars in which England was involved. Impulses towards freedom and progress which the Revolution had inspired far and wide were being countered by an equally strong determination to preserve order and control. Industrialization was progressing apace and generating growing armies of workers, many still in rural situations but more and more of them living and working in the developing factory towns.

The social and political framework of England was under severe strain. To many the preservation of order was the prime concern. To others, freedom and progress were the priorities. Inevitably attitudes and convictions hardened on both sides of this divide, and it was impossible for religion and organized church life to escape the impact of it all. The Church of England, with its established privileges and enormous (and unfairly distributed) wealth, was at the heart of the tensions and controversies generated at that time, but Methodism itself could not evade the shock waves. The story of Primitive Methodism begins in that critical period of English history, and the effects of it were to mould the character of that movement in significant ways.[1]

The spirit of the age

Other social and cultural trends illuminate the changing climate of thought and attitudes of that age. In art, literature and music Romanticism was the dominant influence, countering the established classical style with an urge towards freedom and the fuller expansion of the human spirit. Partly as a result of all this, and partly because of the ugly consequences of industrialization and the growth of towns, there was a renewed awareness of the beauty and power of nature, and of the simplicity and strength of traditional rural lifestyles. This is particularly relevant because of Primitive Methodism's origins in rural or semi-rural situations, and the strength which it was to build up (though by no means entirely) in village communities. It is interesting to recall that, contemporary with the forging of Primitive Methodism, William and Dorothy Wordsworth were expressing in literature their deeply felt responses to rural life, landscape, weather and rigorous walking, and John Clare (the son of a labourer) was describing and celebrating in poetry country scenes and village characters. Watercolour painters depicted the English countryside with affectionate directness, and John Constable's paintings and sketches of his own neighbourhood in the Stour valley of Suffolk were a revelation to many both of the beauty and inspiration of the English landscape, and of the traditional values associated with rural life and labour. In a different way Cobbett's *Rural Rides* and Arthur Young's detailed commentaries on his travels through England enhanced the profile of English rural community life.

It would be quite misleading to suggest that Primitive Methodist preachers, trudging along lonely country lanes, were necessarily thinking of poetry, art or agriculture as they did so! Without any doubt their travels could be arduous, and even dangerous, as is evidenced in the later pages of this book, and their minds were focussed above all on the evangelical campaign in which they were engaged. But it is hard to believe that on their travels they were not stirred by the interest of landscape and the beauties of nature. Indeed the emphasis laid by the Primitive Methodist founders on the importance of 'Camp Meetings' within their strategy of evangelization reveals a deep conviction that to gather for preaching and prayer on a hillside under the open heavens could bring men and women close to God in a special and moving way. And the close-knit community life in both agrarian and industrial villages not only proved to be very congenial to Primitive Methodism but was also in due time to be considerably enhanced by its presence.

Primitive Methodism was first nurtured within the confines of Wesleyan Methodism but was soon to find itself thrust out and disowned by it. This development reveals the strains within the old Connexion in the later eighteenth and early nineteenth centuries, which can be justifiably traced back to the complex personality of John Wesley himself. It was Wesley the pioneer evangelist, the inspired improviser, the recruiter of lay talent (including women), the ardent advocate of hymnody, the popular publisher, whom the Primitive Methodist founders admired and sought to copy. But towards the later part of his life Wesley's conservative instincts had obliged him to attempt to safeguard the continuity of the Wesleyan Connexion by conferring final authority on an all-ministerial Conference (with the Legal Hundred at the heart of it) and by emphasizing the disciplinary powers of the travelling preachers in matters of control over the lay membership. This bias towards control was continued by the Conference after Wesley's death in 1791, and was to be emphasized as a result of the growing discontent and division within the old Connexion.

Methodism could not emerge from these tensions entire and unscathed. The earliest of the major secessions from the mother Connexion, occurring around the end of the eighteenth century, were the New Connexion and the Independent Methodists, though the latter's first Conference was not held until 1806. The Methodist New Connexion opted for a system of government in which authority was equally shared between ministry and laity while the more radical Independent Methodists dispensed altogether with paid professional ministers in favour of a lay ministry, somewhat akin to the Quakers with whom most of the early branches of Methodism (including the Primitive Methodists) had interesting and fruitful connections.

Revivalism

It is clear that there was a ferment of opinion within the old Connexion at this time, and into the midst of this debate over the relative powers of travelling preachers and lay members appeared the fresh element of a new religious awakening. This was due to a spontaneous re-emergence of early Methodist practice, including a revival of conversionist preaching. Among the leaders was William Bramwell, a Methodist travelling preacher, whose convictions and practice as an evangelist were of a distinctly Pentecostalist character, with an emphasis not only on conversion but on the gift of holiness which Wesley himself had advocated as the fulness of Christian experience [2]. Bramwell pursued this particular ministry in the various circuits to which he was appointed and sought to be a centre of unity for the widening renewal movement. He received little support or encouragement from official Methodism, however, which mistrusted any popular movement which might loosen ministerial authority and control, threaten the stability and unity of the Wesleyan Connexion, and rouse government alarm. In this they were proved right. Bramwell's influence was to be a significant factor in the emergence of Primitive Methodism as a result of Methodist revivalism in and around Harriseahead in north Staffordshire in the opening years of the nineteenth century.

The stage on which Primitive Methodism made its first entrance was that part of north Staffordshire

2. I have been at Liverpool etc. – I saw his glory among men; he is still the same God. I bless the Lord, I am saved every moment, and do declare to you that my union with God is such as I never before experienced. I have given myself to continual prayer; and, in this Circuit, I see souls awakened and saved nearly every day. God is working, and will continue to work, glory be to his name! My dear brother, my soul is enlarged. I think I could go through fire for the Lord Jesus. Lord send me: here I am. I have found but very few in this Circuit who know anything of sanctification; excepting a few in Nottingham; but God will come. On this subject several of my dear brethren are more determined than ever. O great God, stand by them, and raise up a thousand to spread the flame.

This Conference has been a poor one. Many were afraid of God working – a scheme to weaken the revival; but it was not carried, nor ever can be. We shall rise above it all. None can hinder: God is king, and shall reign over us. Oh, go on!

Source: James Sigston, *Memoir of the Ven. Wm. Bramwell A Wesleyan Methodist Itinerant Preacher*, Wakefield, *c*.1820, p. 88. The extract is from a letter written by Bramwell from Nottingham in September 1798.

between Biddulph and Burslem, an area of some 30 to 40 square miles. Though not perhaps one of the better known regions of England, it is scattered with place-names full of evocative significance in the Primitive Methodist story. Among these is Bemersley, the location of the Bournes's farmstead, which was in due course to become the publishing house, and effectively the control centre, of Primitive Methodism for some 30 years [3]. This in itself is an illustration of the provincial and lay character of the Primitive Methodist Connexion. The unimaginable Wesleyan equivalent would have been for the Wesley brothers to establish their central base at Epworth in Lincolnshire.

Hugh Bourne's portrait reveals a shrewd, strong face, somewhat dour and determined, yet sensitive. Like his brother James (1781–1860), who worked with him in the founding of the Primitive Methodist

Connexion, his plain attire, demeanour and natural hairstyle (short and brushed forward) are reminiscent of the Quakers, for whom Hugh had a deep regard. This was in due course to result in the adoption of various Quaker-like features and practices by the Primitive Methodist founders, as they shaped their new movement.[2] His upbringing and early environment had a powerful influence on his character which was introspective, scholarly, shy and somewhat quaint, though determined and remarkably adventurous once he had a clear light to follow [4]. His religious experience grew largely out of his reading, but was powerful nonetheless and confirmed his conversion. 'The Bible looked new, creation looked new, and I felt a love in all mankind, and my desire was that friends and enemies and all the world, if possible, might be saved'.[3] Through Quaker influences as well as Methodist he became convinced that Jesus makes himself known in an inward way to those who seek him sincerely, and he earnestly sought to communicate this conviction through 'conversation preaching' and the circulation among his acquaintances of an account of his own experience.

Having become a Methodist almost by accident he devoted himself to that particular cause and placed himself under Methodist discipline. Nevertheless despite recruiting Methodist members and building a Methodist chapel at Harriseahead, he was, before long, expelled from the Methodist Connexion for his persistence in fostering large open-air religious gatherings, under the name of Camp Meetings, which the Methodist Conference had condemned in 1807 as being likely to foster indiscipline and uncontrolled initiatives among the lay membership. The Conference minute on this was brusque. 'Even supposing such meetings to be allowable in America, they are highly improper in England and likely to be productive of considerable mischief; and we disclaim any connexion with them'.[4] It was ironic to Bourne (as indeed it may well be to us) that open-air preaching on the Wesley model should be the cause of his eviction but the anxiety of the Methodist leadership to affirm and enhance the ministerial office, and to

3. *Hugh Bourne 1772–1852*

1772	3 April, born at Fordhays Farm near Stoke on Trent, son of Joseph Bourne (farmer, wheelwright and timber dealer) and Ellen (née Steele). Father somewhat dissolute; mother thrifty and conscientious. Hugh Bourne shy, serious, introspective and a great reader. Brought up in the C. of E., but developed interest in Quakerism. In his youth worked for his father and then for an uncle.
1799	Converted through reading a work by John Fletcher. He and his mother joined a Wesleyan society, and Hugh became a local preacher. By now he was working on his own as timber dealer and carpenter.
c.1801	Through his efforts others were converted, helping to foster revival around Harriseahead. He favoured 'conversation preaching' and lively prayer meetings. 12 July preached his first open-air sermon on Mow Cop.
1802	Built Harriseahead Wesleyan Methodist chapel at his own expense.
1806	By this date, official opposition to revivalism was hardening.
1807	31 May: Camp Meeting on Mow Cop organized by Hugh Bourne under the inspiration of Lorenzo Dow. Despite official Wesley Methodist condemnation other Camp Meetings were held.
1808	17 June: Hugh Bourne excluded from Wesleyan Methodism by Burslem Quarterly Meeting. Bourne continued to raise fresh societies. He published his *Remarks on the Ministry of Women*.
1809	Hugh Bourne published a collection of *Hymns and Spiritual Songs for Camp Meetings and Revivals*.
1810–11	'Camp Meeting Methodists' organized by Hugh Bourne into a separate movement; class

	tickets and the first preaching plan published. First general meeting at Tunstall where H.B. built a chapel (1811).
1812	13 February: the name 'Primitive Methodists' adopted on the suggestion of James Crawfoot. The movement began to spread and grow, as part of the Great Midlands Revival 1816–18. Hugh Bourne's talents as a leader were in administration, editing and writing.
1820	May: First Primitive Methodist Conference at Hull. *Primitive Methodist Magazine* first published, edited by Hugh Bourne.
1821	The *Small Hymn Book* published, edited by Hugh Bourne and William Sanders.
1823	Hugh Bourne published his history of the Primitive Methodists.
1824–5	The *Large Hymn Book* of the Primitive Methodists published and a *Children's Magazine* was begun.
1830	The Primitive Methodist Deed Poll enrolled in Chancery. Hugh Bourne adopted the temperance cause and began to make tours on its behalf and on behalf of the Primitive Methodist Connexion which was quickly expanding. Some tensions between Bourne and Clowes in their later years.
1842	Bourne and Clowes both superannuated on pensions of £25 p.a.
1844–6	In retirement Bourne continued to travel, and visited Canada and the USA.
1852	11 October: died. Buried in the graveyard of Englesea Brook Primitive Methodist Chapel (near Crewe). At his death there were 110,000 members, 5,300 chapels, and 1,400 Sunday Schools.
1865	Posthumous publication in book form of Hugh Bourne's *Ecclesiastical History* (previously published in the *Primitive Methodist Magazine*).

prevent any ventures by lay folk which might raise fears of a threat to public order, has to be taken seriously into account.

A further explanation of Bourne's expulsion is that he had procured a licence to preach from the Stafford Quarter Sessions without the consent of the Burslem Wesleyan Quarterly Meeting, as a Wesleyan ruling of 1803 demanded. The two explanations are interrelated, and on both counts Bourne's initiatives, though aimed at extending genuine evangelical

4. Hugh Bourne was naturally shy, even diffident. He was born at Fordhay's Farm, in the parish of Stoke on Trent, Staffordshire, April 3, 1772, and was reared amid the solitudes of its bleak and desolate moorlands. This geographical isolation emphasized his inborn reticence and may account, in some degree, for the persistence of those gloomy forebodings by which he was beset from boyhood to manhood until his conversion in 1799.

He was, moreover, a very serious youth, in whom the deepest things moved towards silence rather than towards expression. And this again was still further emphasized by the atmosphere of his home. His father – farmer, timber merchant, and wheelwright – though a rigid churchman, had neither the insight nor the sympathy to appreciate the spiritual yearnings of his son. He was, indeed, a hard drinker, impulsive and dissolute, and critical to the point of ridicule of anything relating to Methodism and Dissent. His mother, however, whose maiden name was Ellen Steele, taught Hugh to read, to fear God, and to walk uprightly, though she, too, had little understanding of the spiritual problems of her son; and it was not until Hugh himself had gained the peace and assurance of saving faith that she was led to a like experience under his spiritual guidance.

Source: Benjamin Aquila Barber, *A Methodist Pageant*, pp. 3–4.

activity, were deemed to be outside the bounds of Wesleyan tolerance at that time. When Bourne asked his superintendent minister why he was being excluded from membership the reply was that he had a 'tendency to set up other than the ordinary worship', in other words, that he promoted open-air gatherings and, in particular, Camp Meetings.[5]

Lorenzo Dow

Camp meetings were a feature of North American Methodist revivalism introduced into Britain through the agency of Lorenzo Dow. This is a significant and very early example of the impact of American religion upon British church life, initiating a long history of such influences associated with the names of James Caughey, Walter and Phoebe Palmer, Dwight I. Moody, Ira D. Sankey, and Billy Graham. In these evangelical missions the Americans were returning to us something that we had originally given to them in the eighteenth century, in the shape of John Wesley's Methodism; but what was returned was conversionist preaching heightened and transformed by American revivalism.

Lorenzo Dow (*c*.1778–1834) was an extraordinary product of American Methodism, long-haired, flamboyant, bizarre in appearance and manner, and constantly on the move. In North America he assumed the role of a roving evangelist, 'barnstorming through the Republic at a frenetic pace', to quote Nathan Hatch.[6] His was an extreme version of Methodist itinerant preaching, with all its elements intensified, and focussed in Camp Meetings. These were in effect great religious picnics held in remote woodland settings, with tents as living quarters for the more protracted gatherings. Marching, preaching, prayer, lively music of a folk-song character, shared meals, were all part of the experience. Dow emphasized the importance of full participation by the people in all elements of these gatherings, which were not under the control of an élite of preachers, but open and democratic. The preachers and prayer leaders would employ the same vernacular as the people.

Responses to Dow by the two leading British Methodists in America were markedly different. Thomas Coke was repelled by him, and Francis Asbury admired and encouraged him. In England the equivalent responses to these were those of the Wesleyan Methodists and the Primitive Methodists respectively. An alliance between Dow and Hugh Bourne, who were outwardly very different characters, must have seemed on the face of things unlikely, but Bourne's susceptibility to spiritual power and mystical experience won him over. He had read accounts of what was happening in America in the *Methodist Magazine*, of which the following, by Joshua Marsden, an English Methodist minister, is an example [5]:

5. 'I have heard many say that they never heard such praying, exhorting and preaching anywhere else . . . The several times that I preached and exhorted at these meetings I was sensible of nothing but a constraining influence transporting me beyond myself, carrying me along with a freedom and fulness both of emotion and language quite unusual . . . I am satisfied that they (camp meetings) are the right hand of Methodism in the United States and one main cause why the societies have doubled and trebled there within a few years.'[7]

Source: *Methodist Magazine*, 1807.

Such an account must have stirred Hugh Bourne's soul [6].

6. The social, economic, and political tensions of the years just after Waterloo created a climate that was highly conducive to revivals, but they were infrequent among Wesleyan and New Connexion Methodists. Primitive Methodist revivalism did flourish during the period, and this can be ascribed to the fact that Ranterism fulfilled all the conditions that had generated the 'wildfire' awakenings of the 1790s. For the inner dynamic of revivalism to function well, four prerequisites had to be met: there had to be a corps of effective revival preachers, a desire for an out-pouring of the spirit, a willingness to let decorum fall by the wayside, and some means of communicating revival experiences from one place to another. The Ranters measured the worth of a preacher according to the number of souls won. Women, local preachers, and self-appointed missionaries were all welcome to participate so long as they furthered the 'converting work'.

Source: Julia Stewart Werner, *The Primitive Methodist Connexion*, Part 2, p. 174.

Mow Cop

The strands leading to the birth of Primitive Methodism were therefore drawing together in the early years of the nineteenth century. Revivalism was gathering pace in the borderlands of Cheshire and Staffordshire. Hugh Bourne was emerging as an effective revivalist, discovering the power of corporate prayer and the potential of open-air preaching. As early as May 1801 he preached on Mow Cop near Joseph Pointon's farm, and the seed of future Camp Meetings was laid firmly in his mind. In 1805 William Clowes, the Tunstall potter who was to be, with Bourne, the principal co-founder of the Primitive Methodist Connexion, was unexpectedly converted, and quickly emerged as an emotional preacher of considerable power. From 1804 to 1807 Lorenzo Dow was in England on his first visit, working extensively among the Cheshire revivalists early in 1807, and transmitting to them a growing enthusiasm for Camp Meetings. Hugh Bourne's followers were in fact yearning for some fuller outlet for their religious enthusiasm, and one of them (Daniel Shubotham, a convert of Bourne's) had been moved to utter some words which later acquired a prophetic significance. 'You shall have a meeting on Mow Cop some Sunday and have a whole day of praying, and then you'll be satisfied'.[8] The fulfilment of this prophecy came eventually on 31 May 1807 when the first English Camp Meeting was held, on the slopes of Mow Cop, a thousand feet or so above the plains of Cheshire and Staffordshire [7]. The gathering was an ad hoc mixture of preaching by a varied team of speakers, Independent Methodists, Quakers, Wesleyans and others, interspersed by prayer and singing, with some relaxation and picnic snacks along the way. Hugh Bourne was the principal organizer, Clowes was one of the busiest preachers, on the hill from 6 a.m. to 8 p.m., but the inspirer was Lorenzo Dow. In H. B. Kendall's brief but telling phrase, 'No Dow, No Mow!'

The setting of this story, and the leading figures within it, could hardly be more different from the circumstances of Methodism's first appearance some 60 years or so earlier. In that first story the leading characters were a pair of clerical brothers whose upbringing and education had been forged in a scholarly country rectory, followed by public school and the University of Oxford. They were familiar

7. Again and again Hugh Bourne recalled his people from excess of preaching over praying. In his *History* he complains that in 1817–18 the camp-meeeetings were losing their power, and the converting work had almost ceased in connexion with them. That he had traced to a method that had gradually crept in of holding the camp-meetings 'almost together with preaching and cutting off the general praying services'. In 1819 he put all camp-meetings under regulations which restored the praying services to the camp-meetings, and directed that praying labourers should form in companies and be kept in exercise. Then, he said: 'The Lord returned in mercy, restored the converting power to the camp-meetings and . . . the circuit began to revive.' At the same time 'The people were exhorted, in all exercises, to get as much into faith as possible, and were shown that faith . . . is one of the great main-springs of action in all exercises, that it sets the arm of heaven at work, and that the Lord says "All things are possible to him that believeth".'

There in Hugh Bourne's own words we find the Secret of Mow Cop.

Source: William Edward Farndale, *The Secret of Mow Cop*, pp. 69–70.

ical aims and purposes, were the inspiration of the Primitive Methodist founders and leaders. Wherever they could, they copied his example. The name they assumed therefore was justifiable. It declared that their purpose was to revive and renew Wesley's original Methodism and (by implication) to reject the distortions of Methodist practice which the Wesleyan ministerial leaders of the later eighteenth century had judged it necessary to introduce. There was no major rift in the relations of the Primitive Methodists with the mother Connexion as was the case in the origins of the other Methodist secessions – the New Connexion, the Wesleyan Association and the Wesleyan Reformers. Realizing the unwillingness of the old Connexion to acknowledge their methods and practices, and following the eviction from it of both Bourne and Clowes, the Primitive Methodists simply parted company from the parent Connexion and went their own way, with no great bitterness or resentment involved. They knew that there was plenty of work to be done, and ample room in which to do it and to establish a movement (later to become a Church) which could embody the particular character and aims of the Primitive Methodist founders [8].

with London life and society, and their experiences included a spell of missionary service in the British colony of Georgia in North America. By contrast Primitive Methodism was born in the workaday circumstances of middle England, on the borders of Cheshire and Staffordshire, where agriculture and industry (coal mining, metal working and, above all, potteries) were carried on in close proximity with one another. Appropriately, the founders of Primitive Methodism (Hugh Bourne and William Clowes) represented in their working lives the principal trades and occupations of Primitive Methodism's birthplace.

Yet despite the sharp differences between these early and later manifestations of Methodism there was at their heart much in common between them. John Wesley's methods and organization, his writings and his doctrines, above all his original evangel-

8. Primitive Methodism emerged at a critical time, as traditional culture was fading, but before a new working-class culture had taken clear shape. It appeared just when the effects of economic depression, enclosures, factories, and the putting-out system had convinced many that something serious was wrong with the old social and political order. Ranterism harnessed and transformed into positive action the sterile frustrations with contemporary Wesleyanism felt by numerous Methodists. Although the name which they adopted was 'Primitive', a hearkening back to the past, for those men and women who found their place in it, the 'Society of People' effectively served as a bridge to the future.

Source: Julia Stewart Werner, *The Primitive Methodist Connexion*, p. 185.

For discussion

1. How conscious are you of the influence of the social and economic background to the rise of Methodism?

2. How significant and influential was it for Methodism that John Wesley was a Church of England clergyman?

3. Jot down briefly some of your thoughts and opinions about Primitive Methodism and compare them with your views after reading this book.

2

Early Growth

The Primitive Methodists were strongly impressed by a conviction that the origins and growth of their movement were not of their own making. John Wesley himself had spoken of eighteenth-century Methodism as 'an extraordinary dispensation of divine Providence'[1] and Hugh Bourne echoed these sentiments 50 years later as he reviewed the history of early Primitive Methodism: 'It was begun in the order of Divine Providence', he wrote, 'and not in the wisdom of man nor by the desire of man'.[2] A phrase often on the lips of Primitive Methodists, as they looked back over their history, was 'What hath God wrought!' Indeed these words became virtually a connexional motto, especially at the time of the Primitive Methodist centenary in the first decade of the twentieth century. By then the Primitive Methodists were basking in the glow of their later Victorian and Edwardian progress and their use of the motto had taken on a somewhat complacent tone. In the earliest years, however, it represented an authentic response to an overwhelming sense that their movement had progressed, against all the odds, and in an unforeseen way that could not be accounted for in human terms alone.

The birth of a movement

It was out of the tensions within Methodism that the new movement of Primitive Methodism was born. The powerful motive force behind it was in fact the strong conversionist impulse which stemmed directly from John Wesley's original mission and had been renewed by Wesleyan revivalism in the 1790s and early 1800s, only to be frustrated and repressed by Conference. Early Primitive Methodism was forged by converted men and women who had experienced these frustrations but who had discovered an energizing sense of release from them through leaving (or being evicted from) the old Connexion. They took with them not just a conversion experience inherited from Wesley's Methodism, but the knowledge of an entire system and discipline, forged by Wesley and subsequently adapted by them to suit changing times and circumstances, among which an emphasis on lay leadership was a factor of quite fundamental importance.

It is interesting to observe that about the time that the Wesleyan Connexion was according a clerical status to its full-time itinerant preachers the Primitive Methodist pioneers were sowing the seeds of a major offshoot from Wesleyanism in which lay leadership was to be predominant, and the distinctions between local and travelling preachers reduced to a minimum. There were to be no 'Reverends' in early Primitive Methodism, not even in the case of Bourne and Clowes, or at least in their lifetime. Bourne and Clowes were accorded that title on the medals cast in their honour on the occasion of the Primitive Methodist Jubilee in 1860. Their unique status within the Connexion was, however, to be acknowledged by the bestowal upon them of the title 'Venerable', a term otherwise familiar in English church history in relation to Anglican archdeacons and the father of English history, the Venerable Bede!

What was the character of the movement forged

by the lay leaders of early Primitive Methodism? A survey of the fruits of its first few years will help to identify the principal elements. It is not difficult to recognize in these elements the individual qualities and strengths both of Hugh Bourne and William Clowes; but what is surprising is the way in which the talents of these two very different individuals blended fruitfully together in this crucial and formative period. Just as it was beneficial to eighteenth-century Methodism to have had both John and Charles Wesley as its principal founders so it was to Primitive Methodism to have in its formation leaders as different in character and talents as Hugh Bourne and William Clowes [9].

9. Some Camp Meetings stirred half a county and diffused a new interest and colour into the drab, sordid, and monotonous conditions of rural life. By their means the songs of Zion became familiar to thousands whom the old church hymnodies would never have reached. The echoes of these Camp Meetings have entered into our literature as the works of George Eliot, George Borrow and William Howitt testify. Camp Meetings kept alive the tradition and power of effective, popular open-air preaching. Above all they were instrumental in causing thousands to 'Turn to the Lord and seek salvation.' And yet there are teachers in Israel who either ignore or are ignorant of all this. They will even sketch the history of open-air preaching, and at once – if they be Anglicans – will skip from Wesley to the Bishop of Manchester on Blackpool beach, or – if they be Nonconformists – will take a leap from Whitefield to the Salvation Army. So little do they know, or so much have they forgotten, of the religious history of the first half of the last century.

Source: H. B. Kendall, *What Hath God Wrought*, London: Primitive Methodist Publishing House, c.1907, p. 16.

The success of the camp meetings held frequently from 1807 onwards is a major illustration. The conception was Bourne's, as was also the central place within the meetings of constantly active prayer groups led by experienced and talented leaders whom Bourne loved to refer to as 'the pious praying labourers'. Bourne was sceptical of the value of long preaching which in his judgement exhausted both listeners and preachers.[3] It was in the smaller prayer groups, he believed, and in shared experiences, that conversions were firmly established. Nevertheless preaching was a vital element within the meetings and there is no doubt that Clowes, with his charismatic fervour, was the master here. Bourne's preaching style was, in truth, quaint, since through natural reticence and shyness he tended to keep one hand before his face as he spoke. There was a quaintness also in the content of his preaching. One of his own favourite sermons, for instance, expounded the day of Pentecost in terms of the pattern of a Primitive Methodist camp meeting, pious praying labourers and all.

A spiritual sage

Both Bourne and Clowes, in fact, were convinced of the power of corporate prayer owing largely to the influence of James Crawfoot (1758–1839) the leader of the 'Magic Methodists' of Delamere Forest. A recent writer describes Crawfoot as 'a holy rustic, uncouth and uneducated' but nevertheless 'a spiritual sage' who, according to Hugh Bourne, 'brought forth the work of religion' more strongly than in any other experience.[4] It was through Crawfoot that a strain of mysticism, and an openness to deeply-felt spiritual experience, entered Primitive Methodism, becoming an element within the hearts and minds of men and women who in other respects had their feet very firmly on the ground. It can be said that Crawfoot's influence brought together within Methodism two of the strands of the wider Romantic Movement, an openness to the mystery and influence of Nature and a deepened awareness of the power of inward experience.

It was above all in attending camp meetings that the early Primitive Methodists' minds and hearts were opened to these powerful influences. They knew the exhilaration of marching to the camp ground with lively Primitive Methodist songs on their lips, of gathering in large companies in the open air, and of hearing men and women of their own class and dialect break into prayer, praise and testimony in such urgent tones as to persuade them, the listeners, that they too might open their hearts to the message of salvation, and throw in their lot with the Ranters.

The camp-meeting movement was the dynamo of early Primitive Methodism. It took Methodism back into the open air and liberated it from clerical control and obstructive ecclesiastical machinery. In a real sense it gave power to the people to make of it what they could. There was a chance for a fresh start, with a new enthusiasm, but also with the wisdom and experience of the Methodist tradition to draw upon and adapt as seemed fit. It was literally 'primitive Methodism' reborn but in a new age and a new setting and with new opportunities [10].

---

10. Worship in the open air:

This was practised by Adam in Paradise; and also in the first ages of the world, and under the law, and by Christ and his apostles; and it was revived, and practised extensively, and with great success, by Mr Wesley. This then is another mark of Primitive Methodism and where worship in the open air is not duly attended to there Primitive Methodism is dying.

Source: An early Primitive Methodist broadsheet published from Bemersley by James Bourne, in Rupert Davies and Ernest Gordon Rupp (eds), *A History of the Methodist Church in Great Britain*, 4 vols, London: Epworth Press, 1965–88, vol. 4, p. 379.

Looking back on this story a century or so later Primitive Methodists saw in it, if not the influence of the Romantic Movement, at least a strong sense of 'Romance'. Their interpretation of it by then may have been somewhat coloured by complacency but the important fact was that they acknowledged the presence in the story of Primitive Methodism's origins and growth as something to wonder at, an element of surprise, an awareness of qualities and achievements that are not easily explained [11].

The characters of Hugh Bourne and William Clowes have to be reckoned with here. Both were practical men of the world but had been touched by the flame of an evangelical conversion. This released within them remarkable talents by which to inspire converts and create an organized pattern of communal activity which would nurture new recruits and build them up in their faith and commitment. To begin with the two men ploughed their own different furrows and gathered about them their own followings, the Camp Meeting Methodists and the Clowesites. These developments took place nominally within the bounds of Wesleyan Methodism but the condemnation of camp meetings by the Wesleyan Conference of 1807 brought matters to a head. Taking heart from article 21 of the Thirty Nine Articles in the *Book of Common Prayer* (stating that 'General Assemblies may err') Hugh Bourne chose to challenge the Conference decision and persist in his own course. But within a year the end came and (to quote H. B. Kendall's melodramatic phrasing) Bourne was 'dismembered by the Burslem Quarterly Meeting'.[5] Two years later the same meeting dealt in similar fashion with William Clowes.

The break with Wesleyanism

The movements which had begun to form as a result of camp meetings, and the roving evangelistic activities of Clowes and Crawfoot, could no longer shelter under the umbrella of official Wesleyanism as, somewhat uneasily, they had so far managed to do. A growing company of committed folk felt a stronger loyalty to Bourne and Clowes than to the Wesleyan system represented by the Burslem Circuit and its ministers. The two leaders faced a genuine dilemma, but concluded that their true course lay in persisting with the new work they had undertaken rather than in some humiliating and restrictive compromise with official Wesleyanism. This commitment imposed onerous responsibilities and financial burdens, the latter being in large part carried by the Bourne brothers assisted by other relatively affluent laymen

11. William Clowes 1780–1851

1780	12 March born at Burslem, son of William Clowes (a potter) and Ann, daughter of Aaron Wedgwood.-
1790	Started work in the potteries. By nature Clowes was easy going and convivial. Addicted to gambling, drink and especially dancing in which he took great pride.
c.1804	Spiritual tensions troubled him. Started to attend Wesleyan worship.
1805	20 January converted, with a resulting dramatic change in his lifestyle. Established a prayer meeting in his home and became a Wesleyan Methodist class leader. Began to preach and built up a lively following known as the 'Clowesites'.
1807	31 May. Attended Mow Cop Camp Meeting.
1808	Admitted as a Wesleyan Methodist local preacher.
1810	Expelled from Wesleyan Methodists because of his links with the Camp Meeting movement and lay-inspired revivalism. Became a founder member of Primitive Methodism and one of its leaders and full-time evangelists.
1816–18	Extended his work in Nottinghamshire and Lancashire.
1819	To Hull by invitation (12 January) and took charge of the Mission based there which extended Primitive Methodist work over an enormous area of the north east and beyond, including Scotland.
1820–23	Extensive pioneering evangelism in the northern counties. By November 1822 he reported that 'the ground was all broken up between Hull and Carlisle'. By 1823 Primitive Methodist membership totalled nearly 30,000.
1824–6	Worked in London, Cornwall and elsewhere and continued extensive travelling up to 1842.
1830	By this year it was estimated that one third of all Primitive Methodist members had been raised through the work based on Hull and its Missions.
1842	At the Newcastle Primitive Methodist Conference, Clowes and Bourne were superannuated with a pension of £25 p.a.
1843	Despite illness continued to travel and preach.
1844–6	President of the Primitive Methodist conference. Settled in Hull in his later years and did much work in and around the town, including the leadership of a large Class.
1851	2 March: died. Buried in the 'Primitive Methodist Corner' of the Spring Bank cemetery in Hull.

such as John Smith, James Steele, James Nixon and Thomas Woodnorth. As a result of their patronage Clowes was enabled to work as a full-time evangelist on 10 shillings a week (a fraction of what he had earned as a skilled potter) and a school-chapel was opened by James Crawfoot at Tunstall on 13 July 1811, the first chapel built by what can now be called the Primitive Methodist Connexion, though yet in its infancy. It is typical of Hugh Bourne's realism and practicality that the chapel was outwardly very similar to a row of four Staffordshire cottages, into which it could easily be converted should the cause fail.

By this time the two separate movements of the Clowesites and the Camp Meeting Methodists had come together and issued in May 1811 the first class ticket of Primitive Methodism, bearing this text: 'But we desire to hear of thee what thou thinkest; for as concerning this sect we know that everywhere it is spoken against' (Acts 28.22). The infant movement had then about 200 members, eight societies, a circuit steward (James Steele, whose followers also threw in their lot with the larger body), and two paid travelling preachers, Clowes and Crawfoot, plus the voluntary services of Hugh Bourne, and a dozen local preachers. It might be compared in size to a typical Methodist circuit, but from this modest beginning the Primitive Methodist Connexion was to grow into a nationwide church. The first actual preaching plan (hand written) was drawn up for the four months from June to September 1811 and shows eight preaching places, three of them with fortnightly services only. An interesting insight into the lay spirit of Primitive Methodism can be found in a footnote to this plan: 'If any other person be present whom the congregation wishes to speak, the wish of the congregation must be complied with'. The plan obviously was not sacrosanct![6]

A momentous year in the political and military history of Europe, 1812, saw Primitive Methodism assume its public form by determining its name (see the Introduction) and by publishing its first printed preaching plan. This shows the Sunday appointments of 21 preachers (including Clowes, the Bournes, Crawfoot and Steele) among 34 preaching places throughout the large Tunstall Circuit, stretching from Stoke on Trent to Englesea Brook. The early history of Primitive Methodism was to be dominated by the missionary initiatives of its circuits, Tunstall to begin with, though it had first to overcome a policy of restraint (known generally as the Tunstall non-mission law) motivated by a reluctance to stretch resources beyond what was conceived to be safe limits. The year 1812 was significant also for the so-called New Toleration Act which extended the freedom accorded to nonconformist congregations (though not Unitarians or Roman Catholics) by the Toleration Act of 1689. The importance to the Primitive Methodists of this Act of Parliament is evident through their inclusion of the text of it in their *General Minutes* published in 1850. Primitive Methodism was fortunate in being born in time to enjoy the benefits of the act, but it certainly did not protect the members from severe outbreaks of mob violence nor from malicious treatment by some magistrates, in the early years.

Growth

The movement's growth ought not to be taken for granted, and is not easy to explain. The missionary labours of William Clowes in Staffordshire, Cheshire, Lancashire, Nottinghamshire, Leicestershire and Rutlandshire in the years 1810–18 must be acknowledged. John Parrott, who worked closely with Clowes in the latter part of this period, describes his extraordinary preaching voice 'which produced a most thrilling effect', and speaks of Clowes as a man 'immortalised as a home missionary for faith, zeal and rich success in bringing souls to the Saviour, as well as inspiring by his example and influence junior missionaries and helpers with true heroism in the great spiritual battlefield'.[7] Hugh Bourne's influence was imparted through the organization of Camp Meetings, the printing activities of the Bemersley Book Room (directed largely by his brother James), and the encouragement of active lay involvement in the distribution of tracts and the

12. Not many people shared directly in the early Primitive Methodist experience. Most of those who did were poor men and women living in villages or in towns that had been little more than villages a quarter-century earlier. They were people caught between a passing traditional order and a developing society. Primitive Methodism helped them to make the transition from the old world to the new. Becoming a Primitive Methodist meant affirming that one's soul was important, not only in the divine scheme for mankind, but also to other members of the society. Ordinary working-class people were bound together in a fellowship in which each was given responsibilities and opportunities. A person's opinions counted, his health and his material welfare mattered, his labours on behalf of the society made a difference, his spiritual odyssey during life and his triumph at death would be recorded. Intimate love feasts as well as giant camp meetings brought spiritual drama and song and colour into lives that were otherwise drab. The challenge of carrying the Primitive Methodist gospel throughout England expanded horizons and lent importance to one's own small efforts in a local society. Above all, the Primitive Methodist experience was one of participation in a community of the people's own making, not something bestowed or imposed by their betters.

Source: Julia Stewart Werner, *The Primitive Methodist Connexion: Its Background and Early History*, Madison, WI: University of Wisconsin Press, 1984, part 1, pp. 175–6.

leadership of small groups of seekers in exhorting, singing and the sharing of open prayer. The cumulative effect of this activity in a period of economic upheaval, poverty and social unrest was to generate a strong sense of religious excitement and expectancy which could readily break out into religious revival [12]. The inspirers of the revival which swept through the midland counties in the second decade of the nineteenth century were not only the prominent leaders of Primitive Methodism but also working men and women whose lives had been powerfully touched by an evangelical experience and who were discovering new talents as prayer-leaders, exhorters and preachers. It might be styled a democratic revival in the sense that it was not controlled or engineered from above, and was both an expression of, and a powerful influence upon, the developing Primitive Methodist movement.

Women preachers

In response to the opportunities and demands created by the revival, volunteers were enlisted to serve it in various capacities, generally involving public witness of some kind. As a result the first generation of Primitive Methodist preachers soon emerged, among whom were a significant number of women. A borderline between part-time local preachers and full-time travelling preachers was not at first relevant, but as Primitive Methodism increasingly extended its missionary endeavours beyond the Potteries area the need for paid travelling preachers became urgent, and women as well as men were soon accepted for this work. Wesley had shown himself willing to countenance the use of women preachers, but the Wesleyan Conference in 1803 had turned its face against the practice. Primitive Methodism (and the contemporary Bible Christian movement in the south west) showed a willingness to abandon Wesleyan scruples on this matter. Various explanations can be offered, including the lay character of Primitive Methodism's leadership and the radical influences exerted upon the movement by the

Quakers and the Independent Methodists [13]. Hugh Bourne's eagerness to exploit lay talent in the leadership of the prayer and witness groups, which were a vital element of Camp Meetings, must also be seen as a significant factor, since women were active in this work, and discovered in it their talents for public speaking. In this matter we see a surprisingly radical element in Hugh Bourne's character, springing in part from his strong conviction of the value of lay leadership (female as well as male) in public prayer and testimony. Stephen Hatcher points out that Bourne was 'undoubtedly more radical than Clowes, in character, worship and church order',[8] and it is not hard to imagine how Clowes, a magnificent preacher in the grand oratorical manner, might well feel that the pulpit was a male preserve. In the early formative period of Primitive Methodism there were of course few pulpits and most preaching and exhorting was done in the open air, or in houses, barns, and schoolrooms. In such informal and revivalistic settings the use of women first as prayer

---

13. It is the increased evangelical zeal of the Quakers which helps in part to explain the remarkable affinities which are found between their movement and Primitive Methodism in its early years in the opening decades of the nineteenth century. Hugh Bourne was much impressed by the Quakers and studied their writings and customs closely. Indeed there emerged around Warrington a considerable group of evangelical Christians, whom Bourne visited frequently, who took the name of the 'Quaker Methodists'. Their later history is related more to Independent Methodism than to Primitive Methodism, but what is certain is that Bourne, and others who were to play leading roles in the Primitive Methodist movement, were imbued with a spirit which had much in common with Quakerism.

Source: Geoffrey E. Milburn, 'Quakers and Methodists', *Wesley Historical Society, North East Branch Bulletin*, 35, February 1981, pp. 13–17. See also G. Nuttall, 'Early Quakerism and Early Primitive Methodism', *The Puritan Spirit: Essays and Addresses*, London: Epworth Press, 1967, pp. 204–13.

leaders and exhorters, and in due course as preachers, was accepted as natural by Hugh Bourne, and presumably by many others.

Because of the fluidity of the early period of Primitive Methodism it is difficult to trace the activities of the very earliest women preachers with complete certainty, and no doubt there were some whose names have been lost. Sarah Kirkland (1794–1880) was certainly one of the first, and though not formally 'stationed' she enjoyed the accolade of having been recruited in 1813 by Hugh Bourne himself to be a full-time 'missionary' on a salary of two guineas a quarter, and played a notable part in introducing Primitive Methodism into key centres in the north Midlands including Nottingham in 1815. She married another travelling preacher in 1818 and was appointed with him to Hull in 1819. Suzannah Barber (1776–1851), Mary Hawkesley and Mary Dunnell (fl. 1805–12) were other pioneering women evangelists and itinerants of the earliest period.

This same period also saw the employment of boy preachers. It was not uncommon for male preachers to be recruited into the travelling ministry in their upper teens, and at a time when the Primitive Methodists had no formal scheme of theological training there was some justification in getting new recruits into active service as soon as possible in order that they might learn 'on the job'. Nevertheless some boys were recruited at an unusually early age. The gravestone of Thomas Watson in the churchyard at Warter in the East Riding of Yorkshire tells us that he died in 1837 at the age of 19 after 6 years in the Primitive Methodist ministry. There seems to have been an uncertain divide between a natural eagerness to encourage youthful talent and the exploitation of promising lads for the sake of popular appeal.

Dorothy Graham's researches reveal the names of 125 women travelling (i.e. paid) preachers whose names were recorded in the Primitive Methodist *Minutes of Conference*.[9] Their greatest activity was in the 1820s and 1830s, and the length of service of each preacher was, almost without exception, limited to a few years only [**14**]. The career of the

---

14. Mrs Mary Porteous (1783–1861). Born at Newcastle upon Tyne in 1783, youngest child of John Thompson, a joiner and cabinetmaker who died when Mary was very young. She had to leave school at seven, but taught herself to read and write. Worked in a factory at eleven, then at home. Worshipped at a Presbyterian chapel in spite of the opposition of her mother who died in 1801. Married a seaman, 8th March 1803, and in 1807 became a Wesleyan. Started a prayer meeting, became class leader (1814), visitor for the Benevolent Society, and Sunday-school teacher (1816). Inspired by Primitive Methodist preachers and felt a call to preach herself, though resisted this for some time. Became a local preacher in January 1824, then called to be a travelling preacher a year later, but family commitments delayed this until January 1826, when she was stationed to the Whitby circuit. She worked chiefly in North of England, until she was forced to retire through ill-health in 1840, though serving as local preacher twenty-one years. Died 18th April 1861, and buried in Hallgarth churchyard, Durham.

Source: E. Dorothy Graham (comp.), *Chosen by God: A List of the Female Travelling Preachers of Early Primitive Methodism*, Wesley Historical Society Publishing, 1989.

---

formidable Elizabeth Bultitude (1809–90), which lasted for 30 years, was certainly unusual. The general decline in the numbers of women travelling preachers in the Victorian period was to be largely the result of circumstance rather than a considered and deliberate change of policy. It was one thing to employ women preachers within a revivalistic and rapidly expanding movement, quite another to have women as circuit ministers, occupying manses, and serving a church which was steadily becoming more settled and institutionalized. It is notable that the major Victorian history of Primitive Methodism by John Petty (1860, revised 1880) offers in several hundred pages of dense text hardly any references to women preachers; and, where they occur, the use of an initial for the first name, concealing the sex of the preacher alluded to, seems to indicate an anxiety not to publicize this aspect of early Primitive Methodism.

Another significant sign of those times is an article in the *Primitive Methodist Magazine* for January 1863 on 'The silent power of woman'!

Expansion

The growth and spread of Primitive Methodism in this early period was the result of continued waves of revival, themselves largely generated by great camp meetings. H. B. Kendall, the historian of Primitive Methodism, sums it up thus:

> The note of the [Primitive Methodist] Church throughout this period is aggressive evangelism, and its tangible result was the remarkable enlargement of the connexion's borders. Within the space of some thirty years – the period Luther assigned as the maximum duration of a great revival – a humble Staffordshire mission-Church geographically extended itself from Glasgow to Penzance and the Channel Isles, and from King's Lynn to Haverford West in Wales; and to the Isle of Man and to Ireland [15]. It even sent its agents to the United States and to Canada.[10]

Such development necessitated a constant and ready supply of men and women with the faith, zeal and courage to serve the connexion in many ways, but particularly as preachers. Dr W. E. Sangster in one of his books referred to Wesley's travelling preachers as a 'troop of evangelical cavalry'.[11] The early Primitive Methodist preachers, who travelled largely on foot, might well be described as a corps of evangelical infantry, and their lot was hard [16]. They worked for a pittance, were often at the mercy of mobs and of magistrates, and not infrequently might find themselves confined in some miserable prison simply for preaching in the streets. They had to seek out their lodging places as best they could, and even under a sheltering roof danger might lurk in the shape of a damp bed which could ruin a preacher's health, and maybe kill him. The accounts of the sufferings of the pioneer Primitive Methodists

15. I was called out to travel by the quarterly meeting of Hull circuit in December, 1822, and I entered on my new and important vocation on January 8th 1823. From the day that I left my paternal roof for the work of the holy ministry to the present date I have kept a diurnal record of my journeys and my regular pulpit labours. By the grace of God I have now completed three times seven years' service in the vineyard of Jesus Christ. In three months hence I shall be forty-two years of age. And after having reviewed 'my manner of life' from the period of my accountability to God to the present day, I feel thankful to heaven that I can rationally come to the conclusion that the time which I have spent in the gospel field has been far the happiest, and, notwithstanding, my imperfections, I doubt not, far the most useful portion of my existence. I *feel* that this is not a mean stimulus to be 'faithful unto death.' In the space of twenty-one years I have travelled on *foot*, with comparatively trifling exceptions, 44,936 miles, and have preached 6,278 sermons. The journeys do not include my daily perambulations in the cities, towns, villages, &c., where my lot has been cast; nor do the sermons include exhortations, addresses, missionary speeches, &c., which amount to a great number. Some of my fellow-labourers of equally long standing in the ministry with myself have probably not travelled and preached so extensively as I have; but by others, in these respects, I have undoubtedly been exceeded. So that the extent of my preachings and travels may be regarded as a fair specimen of that of the first race of Primitive Methodist preachers in general. Frequently, after having walked twenty and (occasionally) thirty miles a day, I have been enabled to stand up and preach, or assist at a missionary meeting. Some of my old and esteemed companions in toil are able to confirm this statement. And to their honour be it recorded, I know that they have endured similar fatigues.

An account by William Garner, 1802–1881, a Primitive Methodist travelling preacher, written from Brigg, Lincolnshire, 8 January 1844.

Source: John Petty, *The History of the Primitive Methodist Connexion*, rev. edn, 1864, pp. 572–3.

make heart-rending reading, yet time and again they also convey an irrepressible spirit of fulfilment and joy reminiscent of the Franciscan preachers of six hundred years before [17].

---

16. The small room, a back one, was now appropriated to Mr Flesher's use as a bedroom and study; while the larger one, in the front of the house, served the rest of us for similar purposes, as well as a "living room" for the whole. In this front room we were now become so fortunate as to own a second-hand sofa, bed, and bedstead, on which I and Brother Ratcliffe, and sometimes Brother Thomas Watson to boot, stretched our weary limbs at night in company.

The innocent, exuberant mirth of 'Father Flesher' over the various annoyances of our lot was invaluable. The journeys being long, homes few and far between, and our income too limited to admit of the indulgence of a cab or an omnibus, blistered and bleeding feet were by no means uncommon to us. But if, at any time, any one of "his lads" felt a momentary rising of discontent, impatience, or fretfulness, the glorious countenance and loving words of 'Father Flesher,' if he were present, suppressed the feeling in a moment, and after a mutual hearty laugh, or an overwhelming prayer from his lips for divine grace and assistance, during which tears of joy and resignation would flow copiously from every eye, we would all spring to our feet in an extasy, and grasping each other's hands with holy joy, we would all shout for gladness of heart, and would all feel renewed afresh for the toils and the triumph of the cause we all loved so well. I have sat sometimes on the old sofa, after hours of laborious study to enliven myself and companions, playing the accordion, with them on either side of me vocally joining in the tune, when our spirits would get so excited that we would alternately weep or laugh, or shout aloud for joy. It was thus that we got prepared for missioning to the streets of London.

Source: *Primitive Methodist Magazine*, 1875, p. 172, from reminiscences of Revd Henry Alderslade, Primitive Methodist minister, recalling events of the later 1830s when John Flesher was in charge of the Primitive Methodist London Mission.

---

17. It has often been a matter for surprise to me, that notwithstanding all the fearful examples we have had of preachers suffering from damp beds, there are those who are either so palpably ignorant of the consequences, or so inexcusably careless of the health of our preachers, and the general interest of the church, that they put them into beds situated at a great distance from any fire, and which, in many instances, have not been used since the same preacher slept in them six or eight weeks before. A few months ago I took the week-night appointments of one of our preachers, and after preaching at the last place in the round, I had a candle put into my hand, and was told my bed was in a parlour, which I found to be damp and unhealthy. No sooner had I closed the door than I felt some difficulty in breathing, and such was the stench of the place, that I wished myself away, and would have much rather walked home, a distance of eight miles, than remain there for the night; but it was then too late for me to undertake the journey. I had not been in bed ten minutes before a clammy sweat came over me, and I was convinced that to remain there till the morning would jeopardise my life. I therefore dressed myself, and did as well as I could till four o'clock in the morning, and then bade the place farewell.   Yours in Christ, John Lazenby.

Source: Driffield, 5 November 1853, *Primitive Methodist Magazine*, 1853, pp. 97–9.

William Clowes's missionary endeavours

The first Primitive Methodist to suffer imprisonment for open-air preaching was John Wedgwood who was arrested at Grantham market cross in August 1817. The early accounts of this occasion stress the joyful manner in which Wedgwood accepted his sentence, and the providential results which flowed from it. Sympathy for the preacher generated interest in and support for the new evangelical movement, and a local squire, Sir John Manners, 'took the part of the missionaries and ordered a stone pulpit to be erected on his own ground near the market cross whence they might without interruption proclaim the glad tidings of salvation'.[12] A further unforeseen consequence of great significance was that William Clowes was released from his duties in the Tunstall area in order to investigate Wedgwood's plight and to survey the prospects of Primitive Methodist success in Nottinghamshire.[13] In effect Clowes was given the opportunity to sense the exciting possibilities of Primitive Methodist expansion into new areas well beyond its original birth place, and the result was his emergence as a missionary preacher of enormous talents, whose work was to inspire the expansion of Primitive Methodism over vast areas of the north of England, and in London and Cornwall. In this work Clowes was able to realize his true potential and to stamp on the new movement the marks of his own gifts and character. Many who had heard his name now saw and heard him in the flesh. H. B. Kendall vividly describes the impact he made: 'Until they had seen his eye flash and had their souls searched by the thrilling tones of his voice when in prayer or ministering the Word, they could not be said to know what Primitive Methodism really was'.[14] But there were less dramatic qualities in Clowes which were of service to the movement. Stephen Hatcher puts it well:

> There were features of early Primitive Methodism that were over intense; Clowes was a human face. He was accused of being too lax on matters of discipline, and criticised because he was not a total abstainer. But ultimately his method of loving men and women into the Kingdom brought the greatest rewards. He could withstand attacks because he was so evidently a spiritual man. He gave the Connexion some of the joy that was within himself.[15]

Clowes of course was only one of a growing company of Primitive Methodist travelling preachers in the early passionate missionary period of the movement. The planting of the seeds of Primitive Methodism over widely scattered areas of the country was the work of many hands. Much of this work was inevitably unrecorded but there are sufficient

flashes of light to judge the character of it at a time when the Ranters' mission to convert England was viewed by them as a campaign of the army of God against the strongholds of indifference and sin. There was no master-plan of this campaign, nor was there any one dominant leader, no Wesley. The initiatives were locally inspired and in many hands, and envisaged in terms of the invasion and conquest of new territory where Primitive Methodism had as yet no foothold. Communities which were already well endowed with churches and chapels of various

---

18. When you enter a house wait inwardly on the Lord for wisdom and direction, that the Lord may make your coming in useful, and that you may be preserved from speaking words out of place. Be very careful in making the first salutation or compliments. If the words 'honour all men' be properly in your mind, you will be enabled to show a respect for everyone in the house . . . 'Beware of hasty freedoms: endeavour to speak with care gentleness, and prudence. At the same time, wait on the Lord, that your mind may be kept solemn, and that no lightness or anything contrary to Christian gravity may appear in your behaviour. A preacher should always pay proper respect to the children and servants. Their souls are precious. He should shake hands with these, as if he neglect this, he will be thought to be unacquainted with the nature of Christianity, and in particular with the duties of the ministry. A preacher should certainly wait upon the Lord while in a family, that the unction of the Holy One may attend his words; without this he is liable to blunders and improprieties. The temptations of Satan are quick, powerful, and constant. Therefore, 'let your speech be always with grace, seasoned with salt'. And let it be 'that which is good to the use of edifying, that it may minister grace to the hearers'.

Your obedient servant in Jesus Christ,
HUGH BOURNE.

Part of a letter from Bourne to Thomas Jackson of Belper, *c.*1818.

Source: John Thomas Wilkinson, *Hugh Bourne 1772–1852*, London: Epworth Press, pp. 106–7.

denominations were nevertheless regarded by the Ranters as potential mission fields for their work, and ready to be won. And they were right. In all these places population growth and economic development had run ahead of religious provision, and left an unchurched army of working folk. And in the Primitive Methodists' eyes even those who were churchgoers might not be truly and wholeheartedly Christian. The fields were ripe for the harvest. But despite all the urgency of the mission Hugh Bourne urged his preachers to observe Christian courtesy while visiting families and receiving hospitality [18].

Pioneers of Primitive Methodism

Many vivid stories survive from this early missionary period, often coloured with the imagery of military conquest. Eleazar Hathorn, a one-legged veteran of the Napoleonic wars, stumped his way from Macclesfield to Manchester in 1819 (the year of Peterloo) to take the gospel to Cottonopolis. John Oxtoby (in the mid-1820s) knelt in the snow on Muston Hill overlooking Filey praying passionately for the town's conversion and at last, with the triumphant cry 'Filey is taken!', proceeded there to realize his vision. On the heights of Ashdown in Berkshire, Thomas Russell, a Cheshire man, and John Ride (a convert of Eleazar Hathorn) knelt for hours in the snow praying for an opening into the county, and at last leapt up in faith crying, 'Yonder country is ours and we will have it!' The vision was realized but not without brutal opposition and a three-month spell in Abingdon gaol (including the treadmill) for Thomas Russell himself. Robert Key, a Suffolk man of considerable physique and courage launched a mission into East Anglia in the late 1820s, thereby establishing a strong Primitive Methodist counter-action to the sedition and violence of that area. The passion and urgency of these missionaries is vividly embodied in the story of William Braithwaite, the apostle of northern Lincolnshire, kneeling on the banks of the river Trent and crying out with great urgency, 'Thou must give me souls, Lord. Give me souls, or I must die'. Thomas Batty, an East Riding man who had served on a man of war, was posted by Hull Circuit as a missionary to the dales of north eastern England. It took him time to assess the outwardly dour temperament of the hill farmers and leadminers of this remote region, but after wise advice he got the measure of them. Revival broke out in Weardale and flowed over the high hill routes into Allendale, Alston and Nenthead, and down the valley of the river Eden. Jane Ansdale worked with Batty and proved an impressive fellow missionary in the demanding labours involved. One notable convert of hers was John Dover Muschamp of Westgate in Weardale, a man of some substance and standing, who built the first Primitive Methodist chapel in that community and proved a wise guide to the infant cause. A final lively vignette from the north east is of the preacher Joseph Spoor, a former Tyneside Keelman of somewhat idiosyncratic behaviour, announcing to the populace of the colliery community of Cockfield in County Durham, in preparation for his mission, that he was about to 'sell the devil up and leave him neither stick nor stool!' The courage and individuality of these early preachers cannot be doubted, and would be heightened by their strong regional accents which now we can realize only in imagination [19].

The early achievements of Primitive Methodism were largely due to the commitment, courage and giving of its members with occasional advice and material help from well-disposed farmers and employers. Any interest or practical assistance from the landed gentry was not expected, and relations with them were largely confined to negotiations over chapel sites, or appearances before them at the Quarter Sessions to answer trumped-up charges related to open-air preaching. The outstanding exception was Robert Ingram Shafto (1770–1848), squire of Bavington in Northumberland, who invited the Primitive Methodists to preach in his hall kitchen and was persuaded by their ministrations to join the Connexion, and encourage its work, including Sunday schools, and in due course to become a local preacher. He used to say that 'no section of the

19. For some time past, there has been what I call an extraordinary out-pouring of the spirit of God on the members of our Society; such a manifestation of Divine power, that, unable to support it, they have fallen to the ground. The persons exercised have been various, and the manner somewhat different. Some have fallen while engaged with God in their prayer closets, some while visiting the sick, some under the preaching of the word, some in the time of singing, and some in the time of prayer. They have been men and women, young and old, new converts and old professors; those who considered it the work of God, and those who were opposed to it. A few careless sinners have also been struck down with this wonderful power, have cried to God for mercy, and have (prayer being made to the Friend of Sinners for them) obtained salvation.

That this work is of God to me is very evident from the following reasons: – As far as I am able to judge, all whom I have known to be thus exercised that are members of our Society, are upright Christians, who ornament their profession by an exemplary life and conversation, and as such would not attempt to impose upon their fellow-christians; and they universally testify, that they feel unspeakable happy, and experience their souls to be deeply baptized with the Holy Ghost, as with fire, during such exercises.

Source: William Lawson, *Primitive Methodism Defended*, 1826, pp. 4–5. Lawson is describing events at Brampton, Cumbria.

Christian Church was calculated to be so useful as the Primitives were'. His heir, however, showed no such interest and the patronage of the big house came to an end, but not before Squire Shafto had helped the Tynedale Primitive Methodists to lay a solid base for their future work.

Half a century later, and on the western side of the Pennines, the Primitive Methodists of the Carlisle Circuit benefited from the generous help and patronage of Rosalind, Countess of Carlisle, as part of her eager mission to enhance the lives of the people on her estates through education and temperance. She had a high regard for the Primitive Methodists and is said to have been capable of delivering a very competent lecture on the life and work of Hugh Bourne.[16]

For discussion

1. How would you try to interpret the role of divine influence in the rise of Methodism?

2. Is it any surprise to you that the early founders and supporters of Primitive Methodism were largely working men and women? Jot down some reasons for the answer you give.

3

A Mid-Century Survey

A leap of some 30 years allows us to assess the character, numerical strength, and geographical distribution of Primitive Methodism at the end of what might be called the first generation of its development as a distinctive addition to the spectrum of major English religious denominations. By 1851 Primitive Methodist membership was 106,074 (not counting adherents or Sunday scholars), placing it a strong second to the Wesleyans in the table of Methodist membership, and revealing it to be stronger than all the other non-Wesleyan Methodist movements added together. This represents a very remarkable achievement for what was essentially a lay movement whose members and leaders were largely drawn from the working classes. How is it explained?

Population growth has to be reckoned with. The decennial censuses showed an increase in England from 15.74 million in 1801 to 27.39 million in 1851. Alongside widespread industrial developments this increase resulted in a considerable expansion of working class communities over large areas of the country, both urban and rural, and in those hinterlands between the two which (being generally devoid of adequate religious provision) were ripe for evangelization by the Ranters. The proletarian character of Primitive Methodism, its charismatic enthusiasm, its lively hymns and songs, its simplicity and directness, its vivid preaching and its women preachers, its fervent prayer meetings and love feasts, its marches and open-air gatherings, all presented the Christian message in a manner which to many was entirely new, and to some irresistible. It has to be said that the Primitive Methodists exploited all evangelical

opportunities to the utmost, so much so that a local disaster, an outbreak of cholera, even a deathbed, could quickly become the spark to ignite religious fervour and an opportunity to win new converts. Such tactics might seem strange if not abhorrent to the modern mind and could only be justified if the new converts were quickly introduced to the positive call to practical discipleship within the Primitive Methodist community. Nevertheless it was such expressions of fervour and conversionist activity that explain the rapid expansion of the movement, which doubled in numbers in the decade 1821–31, doubled again 1831–41 [20], and, though at a slower pace, nevertheless doubled yet again by 1871. It was to take another forty years for the Primitive Methodist membership to increase by about one-third and reach in 1911 its highest ever membership of 205,000, after which there was a small decline up to Methodist Union in 1932.

By the 1850s the evangelical movement which had grown out of revivalism in the Tunstall circuit in the early years of the nineteenth century was already a nationwide Connexion stretching from the south coast to central Scotland. Growth posed considerable challenges of how to control and organize the movement, but the Primitive Methodist leaders had as their model Wesley's own system of classes, societies, circuits, districts, and a national annual conference, and on the same basis they founded their new Connexion [21]. It took several years to evolve, and cost Hugh Bourne in particular much travelling and labour, and some anxiety, not least because of his concern to establish the legal standing of the

20. Preaching services usually open with singing and prayer, ending with the Lord's prayer. Singing again follows, (usually short,) after which a sermon or discourse is delivered, for about twenty, or from that to thirty minutes. It should scarcely ever exceed thirty minutes; and the preacher, if possible, should so fully get into faith, as to preach the gospel with the Holy Ghost sent down from heaven. In order to this he should keep clear of all improprieties, all reflections on individuals or societies, and all other unprofitable things; using only, 'Sound speech, that cannot be condemned' (Titus ii.8); and as far as wisdom is given to him, preaching a pure gospel, and nothing but the gospel. After sermon or discourse, the service closes with singing and prayer. The whole service takes up about an hour or an hour and a quarter.

When the pious praying labourers are in proper discipline, (and not addicted to dragging out to too great lengths,) prayer meetings are introduced after preaching, with very great success.

Source: Hugh Bourne, Preface, *The Large Hymn Book*, 1848, pp. vii–viii.

Primitive Methodist Connexion and the protection of its property in law. This was finally achieved in February 1830 when the Deed Poll of the Connexion, in the names of Hugh Bourne, James Bourne and William Clowes, was enrolled in the High Court of Chancery.[1]

The Deed Poll, as well as setting out the aims and organization of Primitive Methodism, also affirmed both the orthodoxy and the lay character of the movement. Its doctrines were declared to be those set out in John Wesley's *Sermons* and *Notes on the New Testament*; and the highest court of Primitive Methodism, its annual national conference, was to consist of delegates elected at the district meetings in the proportion of two lay persons to one travelling preacher (i.e. full-time, paid minister). The same proportion of lay and ministerial delegates was laid down for district meetings also. Quaker influence was at work in these arrangements as it was in the naming of a national conference held by the Primitive Methodists at Nottingham in August 1819

as a 'Preparatory Meeting', which is a phrase borrowed by Hugh Bourne from the Quakers. The Nottingham gathering was indeed 'preparatory' as it set out the grounds on which future Primitive Methodist annual conferences were to be held. Regulations as to the dress and hairstyle of Primitive Methodist travelling preachers also show a clear reflection of Quaker practice. It is not surprising therefore that the Primitive Methodists should from time to time appoint a layman to preside over their national conference. Unfortunately the records do not provide the names of most of the presidents for the earliest decades of the movement but we know that Hugh Bourne's brother James, the Bemersley printer, held this office three times between 1826 and 1842. Only two other laymen are known to have been President: Thomas Bateman, a Cheshire farmer

21. As a Ranter evangelist would have put it (certain) parts of England were a 'field ripe unto the harvest.' That the Primitive and not the Wesleyan Methodists reaped it was owing to trends that developed within the Wesleyan Connexion between 1800 and 1820. In addition to stifling revivalism, for which there was clearly a demand, the Wesleyan conference ignored local opinion, frustrated lay initiative, encouraged social stratification, and burdened poor members with frequent requests for money. Mainly to tighten discipline and so protect the Wesleyan image, the conference increasingly stressed its own authority. This connexionalism forced sometimes trivial local disputes to the centre and pushed central policy out to the periphery, where on occasion it clashed with local points of view. The extreme localism and lay dominance of Primitive Methodism stood in sharp contrast to Wesleyan connexionalism and clericalism. Bourne never chaired an annual meeting. The layman Thomas Bateman, who did so, noted that 'no change of any moment took place [in the Connexion] without my being consulted.'

Source: Julia Stewart Werner, *The Primitive Methodist Connexion: Its Background and Early History*, part 1, Madison, WI: University of Wisconsin Press, 1984, pp. 180–1.

and local preacher, in 1857 and 1867, and William Hartley the jam manufacturer in 1909.

Districts

The original unit of Primitive Methodist organization was the circuit, a large and ill-defined area of uncertain boundaries, and virtually unlimited scope. Some extraordinary mission work sprang from circuit initiatives in the earliest period of Primitive Methodism, such as the Sunderland mission to the Channel Islands (with an eye to the ultimate conversion of France!) [22], Bolton's mission to the Isle of Man, and Leeds' mission to London, all in the 1820s. Hull Circuit was especially notable for missionary endeavours outside its own geographical boundaries. The importance of this period in Primitive Methodist history is made overwhelmingly clear in H. B. Kendall's *History of the Primitive Methodist Church* where 700 of the 1,110 pages of the two volumes are devoted to 'The Period of Circuit Predominance and Enterprise'.

When circuits became smaller as a result of subdivision the district (a regional grouping of circuits) became the more significant unit and was the major element in Primitive Methodist life and growth up to the later decades of the nineteenth century. District meetings had the right to station travelling preachers until 1878, so that many ministers spent their entire ministry within the boundaries of one district, and became associated with it in a unique and influential manner. By the mid-nineteenth century there were ten 'home' Primitive Methodist Districts: Tunstall, Nottingham, Hull, Sunderland, Norwich, Manchester, Brinkworth, Leeds, Bristol and London, and four overseas: Canada (Toronto), South Australia (Adelaide, etc.), Victoria (Melbourne) and New Zealand (Auckland, Wellington and New Plymouth). In the heyday of 'Districtism' each Primitive Methodist district was like a petty kingdom within the wider connexion [23]. Norwich dominated East Anglia, Tunstall the Midlands, Manchester the north west, Hull east Yorkshire and north Lincolnshire,

---

22. EXTRACT OF A LETTER FROM SUNDERLAND CIRCUIT

Dear Brother,

In consequence of an extensive revival in our Circuit, we are under the necessity of calling out another preacher. It gives us pleasure to state that our friends have so increased, that we have not only paid off our old debt, but we have above £20 in hand. Being anxious to employ our surplus money in sending the gospel to others, we have agreed to co-operate with South Shields Circuit (they paying one third, and we two thirds of all expenses) in sending a missionary to the Norman Isles (Guernsey, Jersey, &c.) there appearing to us a providential opening. Several seamen from these places, got converted at South Shields, and carrying the glorious tidings to their native country, excited a great desire among the inhabitants to hear the Primitive Methodists.

We are particularly encouraged in sending a missionary to the Norman Isles, from the consideration that he will not only be supported by much less expense than in England, but we sanguinely hope that he will open out ground which will serve as a nursery for the Continent of France, by enabling the missionaries to acquire the French language, which will soon be accomplished, where both French and English are spoken. From the influence of some of our friends we have already had an offer to take a missionary or two to the islands free of expense, from Sunderland; which we shall gladly embrace, as soon as we have a preacher at liberty. You will, from this, perceive that we are now in want of two preachers.

We are, dear brethren, yours affectionately, in behalf of the Qr. Day,
JOHN PETTY, President.
EMERSON MUSCHAMP, Sec.

Sunderland, 15th March, 1832.

Source: Primitive Methodist Magazine, 1832, p. 230.

---

and Sunderland most of the area which in the age of Bede comprised the ancient kingdom of Northumbria. The outposts of this enormous district included Whitby to the south, Berwick to the north and

23. Duties of the District Meeting

It must appoint a president (and a vice-president) to whom the various speakers must direct their questions, remarks, and propositions, and who must keep those speakers to the business in hand for the time being; must prevent them from intruding on each other when he has conceded to any one of them the right to be heard; must disallow reflections; must maintain the rules of the Connexion when likely to be violated; must impartially maintain the right of each member to submit propositions, and speak and vote thereon; and must submit to the vote of the meeting each proposition (putting the amended one before he puts the original), after it has been sufficiently discussed; himself being the judge of the sufficiency, and leaving the meeting to vote him out of his presidency if his conduct is dissatisfactory to the majority of its members.

Source: Primitive Methodist General Minutes Consolidated, 1849.

24. The 'District Man,' as he was familiarly called, was a product of the system so long in vogue which, as a rule, confined a preacher within the limits of one District. He might by mutual exchange, by becoming a Connexional officer, or through other special causes, find an outlet; but the event was regarded as exceptional. The District Man, old-style, is an extinct species. He was the fine outgrowth of conditions which no longer obtain and can never return. He, probably, like T. Southron, C. Kendall, R. Key, and scores of others whom some will wistfully recall, had spent the whole of his ministry in the District. His interests and preoccupations were centred in it, and his knowledge of its men and affairs and trends of thought, gained by long experience, gave him weight in its councils. He had the peculiar tone and flavour of his District; and if he had any innocent weaknesses and oddities, they but served to give zest to conversation, and were fondly handed down by oral tradition.

Source: H. B. Kendall, What Hath God Wrought! c.1907, p. 64.

Carlisle to the west. The history and character of Primitive Methodist life in some of these districts are lovingly if somewhat sentimentally celebrated in later nineteenth-century books such as Henry Woodcock's *Sketches of Primitive Methodism in the Yorkshire Wolds* (1889), and W. M. Patterson's *Northern Primitive Methodism* (the story of the Sunderland District) (1909) [24].

The fruits of expansion

The adult membership of Primitive Methodism at the mid-century was 106,000, the product of 40 years' growth. At that period congregations at church and chapel included a large proportion of non-members, a fact which is revealed by the result of the census of worship held in 1851, the first and only attempt by the state to ascertain the number of worshippers in the churches and chapels of the nation. Throughout census Sunday (30 March) the total recorded attendance at Primitive Methodist chapels was 510,000, of which 234,000 attended in the evening. These figures can only be regarded as approximations but the census, when interpreted carefully, can be a useful tool, especially when the individual returns for each church and chapel in a given area are examined.

One broad conclusion from the statistics in the census report is that half of the entire attendances at Primitive Methodist chapels in England were in Yorkshire, the Midlands and East Anglia, the heartlands of the movement. The strongest urban concentrations of Primitive Methodism were revealed to be in Hull, Wolverhampton, Leeds, Sunderland, Nottingham, Stoke on Trent, Bradford, Manchester and Yarmouth. In some of those communities Primitive Methodism was challenging well-established Wesleyan strength, and in the case of Sunderland overcoming it by a very small margin, as close examination of the census returns reveals. To have done this after only 30 years' presence in the town compared with the Wesleyan presence of over a century was a remarkable achievement of Primitive Methodism.

It can be argued that Primitive Methodism had the advantage of building on earlier Wesleyan foundations in the sense that the style, language, hymnody and organization of Methodism were already familiar, and part of the fabric of social life of many communities by the 1820s when Primitive Methodism was making serious inroads into the provinces. So to many men and women Primitive Methodism appeared as a new and energetic expression of a familiar feature of religious life, and at a time when the Wesleyans were both settling down into an institutional mode and being challenged from within by radical and reformist pressures. It is important to recall that Primitive Methodism began as an attempt to recover the zeal and practices of John Wesley's Methodism which Wesleyanism was in danger of losing, and as such would appeal to existing Methodists who regretted these developments. The Primitives did not set out to poach Wesleyan members but without doubt they did attract a good many of them, including some experienced and knowledgeable leaders. Bourne and Clowes of course were themselves in this category.

At the same time Primitive Methodism was renewing the evangelical thrust of early Methodism into communities where there was generous scope for its work, due to industrial development, urban expansion and population growth. Such circumstances were to be found in and on the edges of towns, but also in rural and semi-rural situations. So we find Primitive Methodism in farming communities, usually where domestic and small-scale industry were also present; in areas where the mining of coal, iron and lead, and the quarrying of stone, was being extended rapidly; in textile towns and villages; in coastal fishing towns, harbours and ship-building communities. Tin mining is an interesting exception, being largely confined to the south-western extremity of England where the Bible Christians dominated religious life and in effect took the place of Primitive Methodism.

Institutional religion, particularly as represented by the Church of England, was under excessive pressure at this period. Deference and parochial control were being swept away by urban, industrial and social developments, and a radical spirit inspired many working men. The age-old authority of squire and parson, by no means dead in early nineteenth-century England, was severely circumscribed in areas of industrialization, population growth and social change. Working folk were discovering their own forms of association and self-discipline, in Friendly Societies and Trade Unions, and in the chapels and Sunday Schools of Methodism.[2]

By this time the existence of various secessions and offshoots from the old Wesleyan stem meant that in most communities there was some degree of choice as to which variety of Methodism new members might offer their allegiance. It is difficult now to make definitive assessments of the way in which social class and occupation influenced men and women in their choice of which of the Methodist movements to join, but some suggestions might be made. Despite their inherent conservatism and the authority accorded to their ministers, the Wesleyans (Methodism's 'high-church'), had a considerable proportion of working folk within their membership. This may have been in part due to family tradition or to the influence of employers. The branches of Free Methodism with their self-consciously democratic constitutions certainly had an appeal for workers of a radical temperament, but in many communities, especially the more rural, Free Methodism was not represented. To those conscious of such matters the dominance of two lay persons to one minister in the various circuit and connexional courts of Primitive Methodism could be a real attraction, but one suspects that the most powerful appeals exercised by the Prims were the unbuttoned character of their worship, the vernacular enthusiasm of their preachers, a readiness to work in the open air, and the compelling liveliness of their hymnody.

Recognition

Primitive Methodism had its critics but by the mid-century was winning acknowledgement from unexpected sources. Horace Mann, a prominent barrister who was the virtual overseer of the Religious Census of 1851, remarked in the introduction to the Census Report on the evident need for 'aggressive' evangelism among the working classes who were, he wrote, 'really as ignorant of Christianity as were the heathen Saxons at Augustine's landing, and are in need of missionary enterprise to bring them into practical acquaintance with (Christian) doctrine'. Commenting on the value of lay missionaries, and the ability of Methodism to provide them, he went on:

The community whose operations penetrate most deeply through the lower sections of the people is the body called the Primitive Methodists, whose trespasses against what may be thought a proper order will most likely be forgiven when it is remembered that perhaps their rough, informal energy is best adapted to the class to which it is addressed, and that, at all events, for every convert added to their ranks, society retains one criminal, one drunkard, one improvident, less.[3]

A few years later an observant Anglican clergyman working in a northern industrial town commented rather more warmly on the Primitive Methodists in a series of lectures on Methodism. 'They are to my mind the most exemplary of the sects . . . What they have wanted in learning and orderly worship they have made up by abundant zeal in preaching the Gospel to the more neglected portion of the population'.[4] He was even stirred by the example of the Primitive Methodists to commend the employment of women preachers and to anticipate the employment of deaconess preachers in the Church of England!

Chapels

By the mid-century the Primitive Methodists had built or acquired over 1,500 chapels.[5] Few of the earliest have survived the ravages of time, but those that do survive are well worth seeking out. Englesea Brook chapel, nine miles from Mow Cop and neatly built in brick in 1828, is now, very appropriately, the base for the national Museum of Primitive Methodism. The pipe organ, of the same date as the chapel, came from Silsden, and is still in working order. A few miles distant from Englesea Brook is the small Cloud Chapel of 1815, which enjoys the reputation of being the oldest of the chapels built by the Primitive Methodists still in use for worship today.

As a result of urban development early Primitive Methodist chapels have largely disappeared from town centres and are more fruitfully sought in rural areas, with the assistance of maps, documentary evidence, local advice and some awareness of the social and economic character of the area in question in the second quarter of the nineteenth century. In the north of England, with which the writer is most familiar, the Pennine dales which had proved fruitful ground for Wesleyan Methodism in the eighteenth century continued by and large to be equally receptive to Primitive Methodism in the nineteenth, from the early 1820s onwards. The independence and resourcefulness of the men of these dales (mostly hill farmers and leadminers) and the close-knit character of the dales communities against a background of a hard and sometimes dangerous existence, fostered a liking for Primitive Methodism, its passion, its singing and its rugged lay independence. The earliest Primitive Methodist chapels in the north east, stone-built and dating from the 1820s onwards, can be found in Weardale, Allendale and the area round Nenthead, and in some cases are still in use for worship. In this kind of setting a ruin can stir emotions as much as an entire building, as is illustrated by the roofless stone walls of a tiny Primitive Methodist chapel standing in a lonely green valley where two becks meet, at Appletree Shield in Allendale. The chapel dates from 1829 and was founded by John Flesher, then stationed in that area, but its character and situation bring to mind the age of the first conversion of northern England by Celtic missionaries twelve hundred years before.

At Countersett in upper Wensleydale the Primitive Methodists were offered the use of the local Quaker meeting house, and were so satisfied by this arrangement that no chapel was built. Methodists today in that area are glad to continue availing themselves of this same hospitality. The early associations of Primitive Methodism with Quakerism give the arrangement a pleasing significance, though there is some irony in the sharing of a building by two communions, of which one is traditionally associated with noisy worship and the other with silence!

A piece in the *Primitive Methodist Magazine* for 1825, anonymous but presumably by the ever-practical Hugh Bourne, sets out the basic requirements for the connexion's chapels at that period. A central aisle leading from door to pulpit is recommended with short forms on either side, and (if possible) more forms on either side of the pulpit facing inward. Chapels wider than seven yards ought to have two aisles. Pulpits should be at least one yard square and a yard deep, with a Bible board at least two feet long, and inclined slightly towards the preacher. Much emphasis is laid on adequate ventilation by means of window casements, especially necessary in small chapels with a full congregation and candles burning. But such casements ought to be high up to avoid draughts which could harm the congregation. Windows behind the pulpit are condemned; they are 'generally unpleasant both to preacher and hearer, and if the sun happens to shine in then it is disagreeable and troublesome to almost the whole congregation'. Survivals of original chapel interiors are rare, but can be imagined with the help of glimpses based on written evidence [25].

Worship

What was the nature of worship within these chapels in the early period of Primitive Methodism? The preacher could be either male or female, a minister or a local preacher, according to the dictates of the Circuit preaching plan. In the larger

---

25. *Chapel Improvements*

You, Mr. Editor, are well acquainted with 'Mount Pleasant Church', the scene of your former labours. Had you entered it with me on July 18th, you would have been sorrowfully affected, for the windows appeared as if the town had been the seat of war; and cheap as glass was, the reparation has cost us nearly £3. The interior was in harmony with the windows; and the circuit committee thought the emergencies of the circuit, coupled with the recent liberality of the town's society, stood in the way of incurring any expense for chapel improvements. Still the following resolution was passed: 'That Mr. Parrott have liberty to use his influence to get the chapel well cleaned.'

Now the chapel is said to be the neatest in this part of the country. It has about 1,200 yards of painting; the gallery fronts, pulpit, reading-desk, and outside of all the pews, are the best-grained Dantzic oak and varnished; the pew doors are neatly numbered, and the insides of the pews are a well-grained body oak; the eight pillars are white marble; the pew caps, the two vestries, and the inner and gallery doors are mahogany and varnished; also a handsome spring clock is fixed in the gallery; and a lamp is placed in an iron arch over the outer gates, which gives light down the hill leading from the chapel; this is supplied by the meter, and is likely to induce persons to attend our services who, when the nights were dark, were formerly prevented. The labour and anxiety have been very great; but these are passed, the costs are all discharged, and gratification rewards those who have aided in the work. The contractors faithfully and honourably fulfilled their contracts, though their estimates had been low; and the generality of our members, as well as numerous friends, afforded ample assistance; for which we tender our sincere thanks.

Source: John Parrott, 'The state and prospects of Whitehaven Circuit', *Primitive Methodist Magazine*, 1846, pp. 229–30. The Editor addressed at the opening is John Flesher. He had served in Whitehaven when it was an outpost of Hull Circuit. It ought to be explained that the 'Dantzic oak', 'mahogany' and 'white marble' are all the effects of paint and varnish, not the real thing!

congregations a choir would lead the singing of the hymns, and there would be some kind of instrumental accompaniment, organ or small orchestra, to the hymns [26]. Scripture readings, lengthy prayers and a sermon, usually of an expository character, would constitute the rest of the service, though a 'prayer meeting' in which members could participate freely usually followed the service, especially in the evening. Hugh Bourne was particularly emphatic as to the importance of prayer meetings and his instructions with regard to their conduct have been described elsewhere in this book. Democratic in their openness, and charismatic in their enthusiasm, they could form a powerful climax to the entire service. It has to be admitted however that repetition week by week could bring a dispiriting predictability into such services, especially within the smaller congregations. One way of introducing variety into chapel life was the 'protracted meeting', a full day of religious activity and witness prepared for by prayer, and including preaching, much singing and marching, and gatherings lit by lanterns at the end of the day. Hugh Bourne was a committed believer in the value of open-air processions.[6]

The Love Feast

Other special services within the round of chapel life were the Love Feast and the sacrament of Holy Communion. John Wesley's interest in the Love Feast or 'Agape' was fostered through his dealings with the Moravians. It became a regular element in early Methodist worship and was inherited and adopted by the Primitive Methodists. The feast was symbolic, involving the sharing of bread or some other simple food, and of water, drunk from a large two-handled mug, passed from hand to hand and fashioned especially for this purpose. Within the Feast the congregation would join in prayer and song, usually accompanied by personal witness and praise among the members present. The Primitive Methodists were anxious to stress that their Love Feasts were 'conducted on the principles of the

> 26. It will be evident that great caution should be used in admitting musical instruments into the public worship. And none but decidedly pious persons should on any account be allowed to play on any musical instrument, in the congregation, during the time of worship.
>
> With great care and caution it is probable that musical instruments might be occasionally used without becoming a snare. It will, however, require considerable firmness in religious people to keep clear in this matter. But whenever they admit any person, whose life does not adorn the doctrine of God our Saviour, to play on any instrument in the congregation, or to take any part in leading the singing service, they may, at once say, 'THE GLORY IS DEPARTED'.
>
> *Source*: H. Bourne, Preface, *The Large Hymn Book*, p. xii.

strictest temperance' and that they were 'in no danger of abusing them to those sensual purposes which formerly led to their discontinuance', a reference to irregularities in the Love Feasts of the early church resulting in the ban imposed upon them by the Council of Laodicea[7] [27].

Victor Murray was born in 1890 and his account of the Love Feast was based on memories dating from c.1910. The Love Feast had a semi-sacramental character ('a domesticated, democratised sacrament' is John Walsh's description of it) and was particularly valuable as a public evangelistic exercise, often related to camp meetings. If Primitive Methodism in its early period appeared to be more committed to the Love Feast than the Sacrament of Holy Communion this was largely due to the fact that the Love Feast was such an invaluable evangelical aid. Hugh Bourne left it to local societies to make their own decision as to the use of the sacrament, in response to their own members' requirements. It would be a natural reaction for members to desire the administration of Holy Communion once a society was firmly established, with its own chapel or meeting place, and enjoying a regular pattern of congregational life. Hugh Bourne's practical nature is well illustrated by his eagerness to provide recipes in the *Primitive Methodist Magazine* for unleavened bread and raisin wine for communion purposes.[8]

A natural outcome of the democratic nature of Primitive Methodism, and its non-authoritarian ministry, was that the administration of the Holy Communion should be open both to full-time ministers and to lay members, usually local preachers and stewards. This had in fact obvious practical advantages especially in the earlier periods of the movement when circuits were large in extent, and ministers, pulled in many directions, were not always available to administer the sacrament when a congregation might require it. Hugh Bourne was a more enthusiastic promoter of lay administration than Clowes, with the result that in the earlier years of Primitive Methodism more use was made of the practice in the Tunstall District than in Hull.

---

27. The Love Feast:

The Camp Meeting was only one half of the great day. It dispersed with an invitation to everybody to come to the chapel at night, and meantime any sinners who had been converted in the afternoon were usually taken along to tea at the home of one of the preachers. The love feast in the chapel was the culmination of a day of excitement. As there has been an attempt in recent years in Anglican circles to revive the early Christian *agape* as a second best to the Holy Communion and as a service to which *all* Christians could be invited, it is worth noting that among the Primitives the love feast was the chief and most characteristic sacrament. We had the sacrament of the Lord's Supper which was but rarely called Holy Communion and was never called the Eucharist. (We did not know the word, and neither did the Parish church people.) It was a simple memorial service recalling us to the story of our Lord and the deed by which we were saved. But the love feast was our sacrament and was a genuine Eucharist.

Source: Albert Victor Murray, *A Northumbrian Methodist Childhood*, p. 76.

Assessment of the founding fathers

The deaths of William Clowes on 2 March 1851 and of Hugh Bourne on 11 October 1852 were poignant losses for the Connexion but also landmarks in its progress and development. Those who were to be influential in guiding Primitive Methodism into the second half of the nineteenth century, men such as John Flesher, John Petty, Colin Campbell M'Kechnie, James Macpherson, the two Antliff brothers, George Lamb, the three Garners, Robert Key, William Harland, James Travis and others, were born a generation or more after the movement's two founders and while seeking to be loyal to the traditions of the Connexion they were inevitably challenged into new responses by the rapid progress of Victorian society.

Before turning to these developments some reflection on the deaths of Bourne and Clowes needs to be attempted, if only briefly. We might begin at their burial places, Englesea Brook in Bourne's case, the Spring Bank cemetery in Hull for Clowes. Hugh Bourne had chosen Englesea Brook as his place of burial when he was being tended there in illness in 1849, and it is significant that the place is within the original heartlands of Primitive Methodism with which Hugh Bourne, despite all his travels, is deeply associated. Here he had always felt most at home, and from this base the Primitive Methodist Connexion had been largely directed for many years, at least up to 1843. Hull carries equal significance for William Clowes, as the base from which he had sufficient scope and freedom of operation to launch missionary endeavours over huge tracts of northern England, as well as to London and Cornwall. Here in a true sense Clowes discovered his full talents and made his greatest contribution to the geographical enlargement of the Connexion. It is as though he needed to distance himself both from the birthplace of Primitive Methodism and the influence there of Hugh Bourne.

Despite his great qualities, Bourne was in some degree jealous of Clowes and relations between the two leaders were at times strained. One disputed question between them was whether Clowes was to be regarded as one of the founders of the Primitive Methodist Connexion. Hugh Bourne seriously challenged this claim, though later relented. This did not settle the issue, which was to continue posthumously in the wording of the memorials of Bourne and Clowes at their respective burial places. At Englesea Brook, Bourne is described as 'the chief founder of the Primitive Methodists'. At Hull the inscription simply states that Clowes was 'one of the founders', a courteous assertion of his equality with Hugh Bourne.

A refreshingly frank picture of Hugh Bourne's character was published some twenty years after his death by the highly able Scots Primitive Methodist minister Colin Campbell M'Kechnie.[9] There was no temptation to idolize Bourne, he writes:

> He was not intellectual; he was not eloquent, he was not refined . . . his presence and manners were

rough, unpolished, repellent; and yet, as if to pour contempt on human pride, and to show how easily God can dispense with the things to which men attach supreme importance, this very man is elected to inaugurate one of the greatest religious movements of the nineteenth century . . . No one surely will think that we intend to disparage Hugh Bourne's worth or to cast a shadow on his fame. He stands too highly in our love and veneration to render such intention possible. We simply want to strip him of the false, the fanciful, the meretricious.

The same writer observed Clowes preaching in Newcastle in 1844 and gives a vivid account of him.

> He had certainly an impressive if not commanding presence. As for his voice it defies description. Clear and sonorous in its ordinary tone, it rose in times of excitement to thrilling vehemence, more

28. In pulpit and platform efforts Mr. Clowes was incomparably superior to Mr. Bourne. In legislative or administrative ability he was immeasurably inferior. Both exerted a powerful and beneficial influence in the Connexion, but it was in some respects different. Both commanded veneration and esteem by their years, their manly piety, their eminent usefulness, and their high position in the body; but Mr Bourne's influence was exercised with more apparent authority, and with occasional harshness and severity; Mr Clowes' with more paternal kindness, and with a winning sweetness of disposition and manner. Mr. Bourne sometimes erred on the side of severity, Mr Clowes occasionally on the side of leniency. The former had much of Luther in his temperament, the latter more of Melancthon. Their difference of views in certain cases, and the different course they pursued in some matters of discipline, unhappily caused a measure of estrangement between them for some years . . . Which of the two was the more useful, we presume not to determine. Their talents and acquirements materially differed, and so did the sphere of their labours. Mr. Bourne had more strength of mind; Mr. Clowes more fire of imagination. The former had more learning; the latter had a richer command of language and a more fluent utterance. Mr. Bourne took a much larger share in the management of the Connexion than Mr. Clowes; the latter did incomparably more than he in active labours to extend its borders. While Mr. Bourne was efficiently serving the denomination as the editor of its magazine and as the ruling mind in its general committee and annual assemblies, Mr. Clowes was pursuing evangelical labours or home missionary operations with apostolical ardour and success. Both excelled in their spheres of operation, both were eminently adapted to the work respectively allotted to them. Mr. Bourne could not have accomplished what Mr. Clowes effected; Mr. Clowes could not have performed what Mr. Bourne achieved. The Connexion has abundant cause to 'glorify God in' both of them, and to render Him unfeigned thanks for the incalculable benefit derived from their judicious counsels, their extraordinary labours, their earnest prayers, and their fervent piety. They were holy and useful in their lives, and in their death they were not long divided.

Source: John Petty, *History of the Primitive Methodist Connexion*, pp. 428–9, abbreviated (the original source of a piece which was to be much reproduced later).

like the scream of an eagle than anything I could think of. His speech . . . had little unity or logical cohesion; it seemed rather a series of spontaneous utterances . . . presenting things in a novel, beautiful and stilling way. One could not resist the impression that they were divinely inspired.[10]

The contrasted yet complementary character and talents of Bourne and Clowes were excellently observed and described by John Petty, one of the ablest of the mid-Victorian Primitive Methodist ministers, in his history of the Connexion [28].

For discussion

1. Do you think that there is a place in Methodism today for the revival of the Love Feast?

2. Can you imagine Methodist lay members of today undertaking evangelical initiatives like those of the early Primitive Methodists?

4

Becoming a Church

John Petty (1807–1868), whose words ended the previous chapter, can very usefully serve as a representative (admittedly a distinguished one) of some of the major developments within Primitive Methodism in the earlier decades of the long reign of Queen Victoria (1837–1901).[1] He was brought up near Barnoldswick in West Yorkshire where his father, a tailor, offered frequent hospitality to travelling preachers, first Wesleyan and later Primitive Methodist. Among the latter Thomas Batty made a strong impression on the young Petty, who some 40 years later was to publish a *Memoir* of Batty's life and labours.

Self-improvement

Converted at 16, John Petty was enlisted two years later into the ranks of the Primitive Methodist ministry and began the arduous life of a travelling preacher, including a spell on Guernsey where he learned to be fluent in French. One day a minister of another denomination who was travelling with Petty in the same railway carriage asked him, 'Can you read, Sir?' 'I can spell a bit' was Petty's laconic reply.[2] That the question was asked at all must be an indication of the low estimation held by many folk of the educational achievements of Primitive Methodist ministers at that time. The eagerness of the Primitive Methodist Connexion to enlist effective evangelists without close regard for their learning no doubt explains this, but on the whole it was an unjustifiable slur. Conscientious ministers were eager to advance their knowledge and some achieved miracles of self-education. John Petty laid the foundations of his own considerable knowledge by a strict programme of morning study beginning at 7 a.m. and including the scriptures (in English, French and Latin), theology, languages (especially Hebrew and Latin), history and literature. In addition to his religious studies his general reading was commendably wide, including works such as Chaucer's *Canterbury Tales*, Spenser's *Faerie Queen*, Boswell's *Life of Johnson*, Voltaire's *Life of Charles XII of Sweden*, Macaulay's *History*, *The life of Thomas Arnold* (of Rugby School), and Mrs Gaskell's *Life of Charlotte Brontë*. Petty's spell as Connexional Editor (1852–7) is confirmation of his literary ability and also offered him ample opportunity, being based in London, to extend his own reading and general knowledge.

It was during this time that he researched and wrote his *History of the Primitive Methodist Connexion*, a book of some 450 pages which first appeared in 1860 and was published to herald the first jubilee of the Connexion. Petty was commissioned by the Connexion to undertake the task, and all necessary documents were placed at his service. In the book's dedication he refers to himself simply as 'The Compiler', and his work bears the character of a chronicle which pursues its steady way from year to year in much the same determined fashion as the Connexion's pedestrian preachers went about their travelling duties. Nevertheless it is valuable for the thoroughness of its survey of Primitive Methodism's progress over 50 years, and for its abundant detail with regard to people and places. Towards the end

Petty dwells upon the essential character of the Connexion. 'It is substantially a Presbyterian system of government', he writes, 'but contains a larger mixture of the lay element than is found in most Presbyterian denominations'.[3] While acknowledging the influence this has had upon the achievements of the Connexion Petty is eager to stress the vital role played by 'the simplicity and zeal' of the travelling and local preachers, class-leaders and prayer leaders, and indeed of the entire active connexional membership. His words on this deserve to be quoted [29].

---

29. Primitive Methodism has been mindful of the apostolical admonition 'Mind not high things but condescend to men of low estate'. It has usually left the wealthy and polished classes to the care of older denominations, while it has sought the enlightenment and elevation of the poor, the neglected and the downtrodden . . . If its ministry has not been distinguished by eminent learning and refinement, it has uniformly given prominence to the leading truths of the Gospel and has been characterised by plainness, earnestness, pathos and power . . . Simplicity, earnestness and zeal have distinguished the denomination and equipped it for some kinds of labour which, though repulsive to some persons of calm and retiring habits, are nevertheless adapted to the needs of the multitude and have been productive of most important and heart-cheering results.'

Source: John Petty, *The History of the Primitive Methodist Connexion*, 1860, p. 444.

Much of this work had hitherto been carried out largely in rural areas where, Petty urged, it was still needed if the villages were not to be abandoned to 'semi-heathen ignorance, and frightful forms of wickedness and vice', as well as 'the superstitious errors of Puseyism'.[4] Nevertheless he was painfully aware of the call to extend Primitive Methodism's mission into urban communities, where he was convinced it could win impressive results as had been already proved by its successes in Leicester, Nottingham, Sheffield, Hull, Yarmouth and Sunderland. In other large towns and cities, London, Birmingham, Liverpool, Manchester and Newcastle upon Tyne among them, little, he felt, had been achieved:

Does not the providence of God loudly call upon the Primitive Methodist Connexion to assist largely in this godly enterprise – to do much more for the enlightenment and evangelisation of these centres of population than it has ever yet done?'[5]

Petty's vision extended yet further afield into the colonies, Canada, Australia, Tasmania, New Zealand, but it did not even stop there. When these colonies were 'filled with the Gospel light' they could become 'the springboard for the diffusion of Christianity in the most populous parts of the heathen world – India, China and Japan'. Petty was allowing himself here to be swept along on a high tide of Victorian optimism. Nevertheless large areas of his vision of Primitive Methodism's further extension and progress at home and abroad were to be substantially realized by the end of the century.

This progress ought not to be taken for granted. It was by no means clear in the 1830s and 1840s what course Primitive Methodism might take. As a conversionist movement with a membership largely recruited from the working classes, and a lowly-paid ministry with no formal training and outnumbered by lay members in the ratio of two to one in all the significant courts of the Connexion, both local and national, its achievements and aspirations might well have been limited to that of a revivalist movement largely lay in character, and aimed primarily at the conversion and Christianizing of agricultural and industrial labourers and their families. This work itself was important enough, but was not regarded by the wiser Connexional leaders as an end in itself. Alongside evangelism there was from the beginning of the movement, and springing largely from the example of Hugh Bourne, a serious concern for things of the mind and for the enlargement of knowledge and understanding. Travelling preachers of a studious cast of mind, long before the establishment of a Primitive Methodist theological college, performed miracles of self-education by a strict discipline with regard to regular times of study. The stimulus of lively and intelligent members among their congregations was an important factor in all this. John Petty himself was a notable product of this process, and a fervent advocate of ministerial study and theological training within Primitive Methodism.[6]

Before enlarging on that theme, and concern for things of the mind, we need to return to the fundamental impulse of Primitive Methodism, that is the call to mission, no longer confined to 'home mission' within the British Isles, but extending to missionary ventures overseas.

Overseas missions

In its early period all Christian work which Primitive Methodism initiated was conceived in missionary terms, whether the venture was aimed at a neighbouring village or the other side of the globe.[7] Moreover while some missionary initiatives were launched in the name of the Connexion others were the fruit of chance or of individual ventures. North America illustrates both processes well. Four missionaries sailed for New York in 1829. One of them was Ruth Watkins, the first Primitive Methodist woman to be commissioned to work overseas, and she was followed a year later by her brother Nathaniel. Both had already served briefly as travelling preachers in English circuits. Within a decade or so scattered Primitive Methodist societies resulting from this work united to form the Primitive Methodist Church in North America, which by 1900 had 100 churches and nearly 7,000 members. By contrast Primitive Methodist work in Canada was planted through the personal initiative of William Lawson, a layman from Brampton in the Carlisle circuit, who with his wife Ann emigrated there in 1829, to be followed soon after by one of his employees, Robert Walker. Walker succeeded to Lawson's business in Toronto and prospered sufficiently as to become a generous donor to Canadian Primitive Methodism. 'Few men have done so much to extend Primitive

Methodism in Canada' says his biographer.[8] Under more formal arrangements John Davison, Clowes's son-in-law and biographer, went to Canada in 1847 as Secretary to the first Canadian Primitive Methodist Conference at Brampton, Ontario, in 1854. Another English Primitive Methodist minister, Thomas Guttery, conducted an impressive eight-year ministry in Toronto in the 1870s. By 1883 Canadian Primitive Methodism was able to contribute over 8,000 members and 99 travelling preachers to the newly united Canadian Methodist Church.

The 1840s saw the formal missioning by the Primitive Methodists of Australasia, though the earliest settlers had included some lay members of the Connexion who sought to plant the seeds of Primitive Methodism in their colonial setting. The impulse to mission New Zealand was the result of a historic gathering in 1843 at the Primitive Methodist chapel in Cramlington, Northumberland, where the idea of a mission to the Southern hemisphere, supported by

---

30. The New Zealanders are much excited about the land question, and their general topic is war. They have broken up a small settlement where two Scotch missionaries were stationed, and had been labouring among the natives for upwards of two years. The missionaries were amongst the last persons who fled, and they were compelled to leave for the safety of their lives. Since they left, nearly every house belonging to the few European settlers has been burnt down; and at a settlement about seventy miles from Wellington, on the way to New Plymouth, the natives have massacred nearly the whole of a large family, and robbed many of the settlers, burning their corn, and driving away their cattle. New Plymouth is now in peril, as the natives are determined to fight for the land there. I feel much for Dear Brother Ward and his family, as there is no military force at the place nor place of refuge whither the inhabitants can fly for safety; and there are but eleven hundred Europeans, including women and children.

Source: 'Primitive Methodist Missionary Notices', No. li for January 1848 from Henry Green, *Primitive Methodist Magazine*, 1848.

subscriptions from the Connexion's Sunday schools, was first broached. The vision was soon realized when Robert Ward, a travelling preacher with a decade's experience in East Anglian circuits, sailed out with his wife Emily to found a Primitive Methodist mission in New Plymouth, New Zealand in 1844.

The challenges were formidable [30] but Ward went on to serve in the antipodes for a quarter of a century, establishing new Primitive Methodist stations at Auckland, Wellington and Christchurch. In 1913 3,400 Primitive Methodists from New Zealand joined in the united Methodist Church of Australasia.

Lay initiatives from around 1840 led to the founding of Primitive Methodism in Australia, at Port Adelaide, and in due course at Sydney, Melbourne, Victoria and other places. Tasmania was missioned by East Anglian emigrants in 1858. British ministers were formally stationed in Australia and New Zealand from the mid-1850s and some of them remained to work out their entire ministry there. Australasia was to attract some of British Primitive Methodism's ablest travelling preachers, who relished the frank, intelligent and radical character of their congregations. Men like Hugh Gilmore (1842–91) found their fullest and most satisfying ministry in Australia, 'Statesmen, judges, editors, and literary men of all grades attended his ministry, and the common people heard him gladly', wrote his fellow minister and friend, Joseph Ritson, of Gilmore's all too brief ministry in North Adelaide[9] [31]. Gilmore's successor at Adelaide was John Day Thompson who exceeded Gilmore in his boldly radical convictions, political and theological. At the 1896 Primitive Methodist Conference at Burnley he was even charged with heresy, but was cleared and went on to enjoy several key positions within the Primitive Methodist establishment, including the presidency in 1915.

---

31. The North Adelaide Church, now that a gallery has been put into it [by Gilmore] is commodious and splendidly situated, and the people were prepared to give their confidence to a true man. His congregations were overflowing from the first. Artisans, professional men, statesmen, crowded his ministry; Agnostics and Socialists, who had not darkened a church-door for years, sat alongside of men of different creeds. Each man felt that there was a preacher who had a message for them. The pulpit was the great power he wielded, but, as in England, his energies ran out in various directions. All the Churches laid his services under contribution for special occasions, and crowds came whatever church he was in. He was literally always at work. He was an enthusiast in the advocacy of Land Nationalisation; then he became an ardent worker in the Single Tax Crusade. Not only did he preside at Mr Henry George's own meetings; he strove with all his might to spread his economic doctrine by personal persuasion and by lectures, speeches, and classes. For a time he edited the *Pioneer*, the Single Tax organ, and wrote much for its columns, he was also President of the League. The celebrated Sir George Grey presided at one of his lectures, and was so much impressed that at the close he paid the highest tribute that one man can pay another. He said: 'I have never heard an address so eloquent, arguments so cogent, or seen an audience so moved.' Another chairman said he was the 'finest speaker in Australia.'

Source: H. B. Kendall, *The History of the Primitive Methodist Church*, vol. 2, pp. 434–5.

Africa

There was something natural and inevitable in the extension of Primitive Methodism to those parts of the Empire settled largely by British colonists, and it has to be remembered that missionary work in the British colonies was aimed not only at the natives but also at the settlers themselves, who, having left behind the social structures and constraints of life in England, could, in H. B. Kendall's words, throw off whatever Christian civilization had given them and show 'a tendency to revert to rudeness'! Africa, and especially West Africa, was a challenge of a different dimension. As early as 1837 the missioning of West

Africa was bravely advocated at the Primitive Methodist Conference, but it was over 30 years later that Richard William Burnett and Henry Roe sailed out in the aptly named *Pioneer* to Fernando Po (now called Bioko), a Spanish-owned island in the Bight of Biafra. Henry Roe later wrote two books, *West African Scenes* (1874: on Fernando Po) and *Mission to Africa*, on the first Primitive Methodist missionary work there, published about the same date. They landed, on 21 February 1871, after nearly four weeks at sea, to commence their mission on an island some 44 miles by 20 miles, with a mean temperature of about 80°F and a population consisting of several hundred Europeans (mainly Spanish) and some 23,000 Bantu natives. They were not in fact the very first Primitive Methodist missionaries on Fernando Po, since, true to the Connexion's lay character two Primitive Methodist sailors (a ship's master and carpenter) had preached to the native islanders here a year and a half earlier. And there is an appropriate homeliness in the names of Mamma Job (a redeemed slave) in whose house Roe and Burnett led their first service, and of William Napoleon Barleycorn, one of their first native recruits who went on to serve as a minister for 40 years, and also trained as a teacher [32]. Another redeemed slave (Peter Bull) acted as an interpreter. The island in fact had become a refuge for redeemed slaves, many West Indians among them. It also served in due course as a base for Primitive Methodist missionary work in Eastern Nigeria, where James Marcus Brown established a mission at Acqua River in 1894, and where a Training Institute to equip native teachers was established. Early in the twentieth century Frederick Dodds, a Primitive Methodist minister, undertook pioneering work among the Ibo people for a period of over 30 years, and was Chairman of the Primitive Methodist district in Eastern Nigeria when it united with Wesleyan Methodist work in Western Nigeria as a result of Methodist Union.

Other Primitive Methodist missionary ventures were scattered over the vast territories of southern Africa. These were primarily: Aliwal North on the Orange River where Henry Buckenham was the pioneer (1871–6) and where George E. Butt and his son served for 17 years (1888–1905); Nkala in Northern Rhodesia; and Masukulumbweland in the Zambezi area, where Henry Buckenham was again the pioneer missionary in the 1890s aided by Arthur Baldwin and others. This last venture was a deliberate attempt to launch a mission in 'the clear, open field of untouched heathenism' and the difficulties and challenges were great [33]. Challenges of a different kind were faced on Fernando Po at Santa Isabel, the principal settlement, where the missionaries were especially vulnerable to interference and opposition from certain prejudiced Spanish governors.[10] William Holland was there in the early 1890s and was treated in such a scandalous way that the Spanish Government itself felt obliged to disown the governor's action. Primitive Methodist mission

---

32. From the beginning William Napoleon Barleycorn (1848–1925) showed rare promise. He became an assistant class leader to Henry Roe and accompanied him on many an itinerary to the native villages. In 1871 he was added to the Fernandian mission staff and assisted the Revd D. T. Maylott in opening the San Carlos mission. His European brethren trusted him. He was a brother, loyal and devoted, and nursed the Revd R. S. Blackburn at San Carlos and was with him to the end. He became a minister of our Church in 1884 and threw himself more whole-heartedly into winning his fellow Africans to Christ. He qualified as a Spanish school teacher, but an unfriendly Governor of Fernando Po repudiated his qualifications. About 1895 he took charge of the Banni Station and laboured there for 23 years among the native Bubis as their spiritual father. On his visits to England he endeared himself to all. In the homes of our people he showed himself to be what he always was, a Christian gentleman. He invariably gave the Mission staff wise counsel and advice and to the end was intellectually vigorous and kept pace with the times in thought and outlook. Not only is Santa Isabel the poorer for his loss, but the whole of Africa. She can ill spare such men.

Source: W. N. Barleycorn's obituary in *Primitive Methodist Minutes*, 1926, pp. 255–7.

33. The missionary party left Aliwal North in December for Kimberley. There was a delay of several weeks on account of the non-arrival of stores consequent on a dockers' strike in London. They began their journey from Kimberley in March, 1890, in three well-loaded waggons, each drawn by eighteen oxen, and a cart drawn by six. They had difficulties in travelling from the start, the waggons almost daily sticking fast in the clayey ground or deep sands, requiring great labour to extricate them . . . It took three months to go from Palapye across the Kalahari Desert to the Zambesi. It was a toilsome journey, beset with hardships, perils and privations, including suffering through the failure of water supplies, but at last they reached the river, when greater trials and disappointments awaited them . . . On their journey they were caught by the floods, and Mr Baldwin and his colleagues were compelled to take refuge on an ant-hill which formed an island in the midst of the inundated land. Here, amid ants and mosquitoes, and with nothing to shelter them save a waggon cover, they were compelled to remain several weeks until the waters had subsided.

Source: James Travis, *Seventy Five Years*, pp. 117–18.

schools were closed, singing in the chapels was forbidden, native members of the mission were subject to much harassment, Holland himself was imprisoned, and finally he and his wife were banished from the island.[11]

The total number of Primitive Methodist overseas missionaries was never great at any one period. By the mid-1920s there were six in Northern Rhodesia, eight in Nigeria, six in Fernando Po and other West African stations, and two in South Africa. Yet the financial costs of missionary work weighed heavily on the Connexion. To quote again from the mid-1920s, expenditure on African missions was £10,000 more than the relative income.[12]

Education and improvement

This section begins with a pleasant example of the inter-relatedness of the varied aspects of Primitive Methodism's life and work. On Thursday 29 September 1887, William Napoleon Barleycorn, while on a visit to this country, was a guest at Bourne College, Quinton, in the city of Birmingham, one of the three secondary boarding schools founded in England by the Primitive Methodist Church.[13] He sang to the boys in his own native tongue and obviously enjoyed himself. In due course Mr Barleycorn's son Rowland was to enter the school as a pupil. Bourne College was in fact a product of a campaign within Primitive Methodism advocating secondary and college education. John Petty was one of its most vocal and influential leaders. In 1860 he had urged the Connexion to deploy its Jubilee Fund (raised to show gratitude for Primitive Methodism's life and work over 50 years) on behalf of four major causes – chapel building, missions, a Connexional boarding school, and improved education for ministerial candidates and young ministers [34]. The first two

34. The rapid advancement of popular education in our age and country calls for a higher degree of pulpit qualification. To say nothing of the press, which is making an impression on the public mind wholly unprecedented in the history of our world, the instruction given to the millions in our Sabbath-schools, and the large augmentation of the means of general tuition, have created a capacity for knowledge, and awakened a spirit of inquiry, which may prove favourable to the cause of Christ, or otherwise, just as the ministry shall be correspondingly enlightened and energetic, or common-place and stationary. No minister, now, can rationally hope to gain and retain the attention and respect of his congregation by trite generalities, loud declamation, empty witticisms, and either ludicrous or pathetic anecdotes. Lucid and ample instruction, just and forcible reasoning, appropriate and striking illustration, direct, as well as earnest, address, are more urgently and generally demanded than at any former period.

Source: William Dent (1806–84) (Primitive Methodist Minister) from an article on 'The importance of an enlightened ministry', *Primitive Methodist Magazine*, 1857, p. 349.

causes were already generally accepted throughout the Connexion so Petty set himself to urge the importance of education [35]. About the time of the Jubilee the Primitive Methodist Conference had urged that in addition to Sunday schools and evening schools, Primitive Methodist day schools should be established as widely as possible. Nevertheless it was accepted that the Jubilee Fund should be used particularly to provide the Connexion with what was described as a 'middle class public school' for the children of those members who could afford to send them there, and (at reduced fees) for ministers' children whose education was often seriously disrupted by the consequences of ministerial stationing.

Petty had his finger on the Connexion's pulse in these matters. Social elevation as a consequence of evangelical disciplines and a puritan lifestyle is a familiar feature in social history, and it certainly was to be seen in Primitive Methodism.[14] This is not to say that many members of the Connexion were becoming rich (though some were) but they certainly had rising educational and cultural expectations with regard to themselves and their children, and, it has to be said, with regard to the quality and training of their ministers also. In the early decades of the Connexion's history young recruits into the Primitive Methodist ministry served up to four years

---

35. Need for changes in preaching style and content

If some of the holy and honoured men who accomplished such wonders during the Connexion's infancy were still living amongst us, with the acquirements they then possessed, would their zeal and piety atone for their lack of education? Would our intelligent friends (i.e. adherents) willingly sit under their ministry? Do not our people generally require something for thought? . . . Unless we meet this challenge we shall have the mortification of seeing the intelligent part of our people, the young especially, deserting our ministry for one of higher attainments, and better qualified to *teach*.

Source: *Primitive Methodist Magazine*, 1864, p. 466.

---

36. Again, allow me to remind you that a considerable amount of prejudice prevails in our denomination, as in some others, against ministerial colleges, or theological institutions. And though many who imbibe this prejudice may be persons of narrow minds, of next to no education, and, perhaps, of superficial piety, yet this is far from being the case with *all* who look upon institutions of this kind with a jealous eye. In many cases the jealousy entertained is 'a godly jealousy,' though possibly mixed with human infirmity and mistaken views. In these cases the persons are not only to be borne with but respected and esteemed as their excellences demand. And in *no case* should the opponents of such institutions be despised, or treated with rudeness or disrespect, but with Christian forbearance, brotherly kindness, and a tender regard to their feelings and views. The best way to overcome their prejudice is *to live it down*, to overcome it by your exemplary behaviour and Christ-like spirit. Instead of being proud, conceited, and superficial young men (as many of our pious people fear you may be) piquing yourselves upon having been at college, and acquired a smattering of human learning, seek, my brethren, a baptism of the Holy Spirit, such a conformity to the lovely image of the Saviour, such intimate and daily communion with God, that on leaving the institution, you may show by your humility and lowliness of mind, your docility and meekness, your deeply devout and prayerful spirit, and your earnest consecration to your great work, that *you*, at least, have not been spoiled by coming to the institution, but that your religious improvement has, at least, been equal to your improvement in knowledge and ministerial gifts.

Source: John Petty, *Systematic Theology*, ed. Colin Campbell M'Kechnie, London, 1874, pp. 14–15.

---

probationary training, under the guidance of an experienced travelling preacher, with an examination before the relevant District Committee at the start of the process, and once again at the end when, if all had gone well, they were 'admitted into full connexion', that is into full orders. The more scholarly ministers such as John Petty were aware of the inadequacy of these arrangements and at the same time conscious of a reluctance within the Connexion to approve a theological college [36]. Perhaps a way forward could be found by bringing together the establishment of a boarding school with the provision of training for candidates for the Primitive Methodist ministry?

In January 1864 the Primitive Methodist Jubilee School for boys, otherwise known as Elmfield College, opened in premises on the Malton Road, York. John Petty was appointed as its Governor and his wife as Matron; J. K. Dall, B.A., was head master. Within a dozen years two more Connexional boarding schools were opened by the Primitive Methodists, the Ladies College at Clapham, London (1874), and Bourne College for boys at Quinton, Birmingham (1876).[15] The former was short lived, but Quinton was active to 1928 [37]. Elmfield outlived both, and in 1932 was united with another Methodist school, Ashville, at Harrogate, which still lives on as a boarding and day school for over 800 boys and girls. Inadvertently Elmfield was to have a place in the story of Primitive Methodist ministerial training. Resulting from the unexpected availability of empty rooms at the school, an important development took place in 1865 when a group of young

ministerial candidates was accepted into Elmfield to train for one year under Petty's tutorship. Some fifty men altogether were to train in this way over the next three years, including Thomas Mitchell, a future Connexional Book Steward (with general oversight of Primitive Methodist printing and publishing) and President of the Primitive Methodist Conference.

Ministerial training

However, the forceful protagonists of ministerial training (notably the highly able and scholarly ministers James Macpherson and Colin Campbell M'Kechnie – both Scots) regarded the use of Elmfield merely as a makeshift. They had both invested too much of their careers in promoting the cause of ministerial education, M'Kechnie in the Sunderland Primitive Methodist District, and Macpherson mainly in the Manchester District, to accept any final outcome that fell short of a properly established training institution.[16] It is significant that Macpherson had worked very closely with John Petty in Sunderland and the Channel Islands at the start of his ministerial career, and much later was to publish a revised and extended version of Petty's history of the Connexion. Both he and M'Kechnie shared Petty's own strong conviction that authentic ministerial training must combine spiritual and intellectual elements. Anything less than this would never have found acceptance by Conference and the Connexional membership in general, among whom there was a considerable element who regarded a college as a dubious and expensive luxury. Nevertheless it has to be said also that developments within the Connexion (and within society at large) in the third quarter of the nineteenth century were conspiring to provoke a desire for more social and cultural stimulus from chapel life and worship than had hitherto been recognized. This period of English history has been designated as 'the age of improvement' and religious activity, social as well as devotional, was caught up in the wider mood.

---

37. Bourne College brought new blood and new talent into the village, and there was a very real sense in which it also brought the world to Quinton. During the forty-seven years of its existence in the village, 1,198 boys (of whom 39 came from Quinton) were educated at Bourne College. They came from Welshpool to Warrington, from Berwick-on-Tweed in the north to Redruth in the south, from parts of the world as diverse as France, British Guinea and that favourite preaching ground of Primitive Methodist missionaries, Fernando Po, from where Revd Napoleon Barleycorn sent his sons to Quinton to be educated. The impact upon the little community of farm labourers, shop-keepers and small-time metal-workers was enormous as the college brought new life to the village in those pivotal years around the end of the nineteenth century.

Source: Michael Hall, *Ravers, Ranters and Respectable Schoolboys*, 1981 and 2001.

Primitive Methodism itself was experiencing change and development, and becoming a substantial and respected element in the ecclesiastical life of many communities. New and improved chapels were being built, many of them following suburban development out from the older crowded town centres. The Connexional magazines were improving markedly in character and content, and a new hymn book had replaced the early collections. A younger generation of Primitive Methodist members, lively and critical, was restive with a desire for teaching and preaching that was intelligent and meaningful. Accompanying these developments was a stronger sense of Connexionalism with a corresponding awareness that Primitive Methodism was assuming the character of a church, and bearing the responsibilities of maintaining a worthy and dignified aspect to society in its worship and congregational life.

The role and deployment of the ministry were central to this process. One significant development from the mid-century onwards was a deliberate policy to subdivide the older sprawling circuits, especially in populous urban communities. This limited the number of chapels that ministers preached in so that they faced the same congregations much more frequently than before. Their role was becoming increasingly that of pastor and teacher, and less that of travelling evangelist. Their preaching would have to be more varied, more instructive, more thoughtful, for which hard study and clear thinking were essential. Preachers, especially ministers, needed more training and instruction if they were to be up to their job.

At this period Primitive Methodism was essentially a union of semi-independent districts. Connexionalism was weak. It is not therefore surprising that the first major developments in ministerial training sprang from two districts, Manchester and Sunderland, nor that the key figures in this process were James Macpherson and Colin M'Kechnie, both of whom had benefited from the Scottish educational system and had a strong inclination towards scholarship which they were eager to exercise and encourage within Primitive Methodism. M'Kechnie was a remarkably talented minister, one of the most able and impressive in the central period of the Connexion's history, if not of its entire span. In his scholarship, and his powerful influence as a generator of religious revivals in the Circuits in which he worked, he might almost be said to have been blessed with the contrasted but complementary talents of both Bourne and Clowes. To him there was no conflict between intellectuality and evangelical religion, and he was eager to promote this conviction in practical ways. He loved talking on religion with lively minded young people in the north eastern circuits in which he worked – coal miners in the pit villages, artisans in the mechanics institutes, and alert young women in their Bible classes. Above all he had an acute longing to enlarge ministers' minds and equip them more fully for their pastoral and teaching responsibilities.

M'Kechnie was the instigator in 1850 of the Sunderland District Ministerial Association which met for three days each year after the District May Meeting, and introduced a tutorial system by which experienced ministers could assist their younger colleagues in their studies. An important result of these developments was the launching of the *Christian Ambassador*, a remarkably progressive quarterly journal edited by Colin M'Kechnie for the publication of the papers read at the Association's meetings. The *Ambassador* was a highly effective medium through which to promote the cause of theological education, especially within the Sunderland District but not confined to it. In due course it became a connexional publication as the *Primitive Methodist Quarterly Review*, later *The Holborn Review*.

The Sunderland College

Contemporary with these developments in the north east, a system of training probationer ministers was launched in the Manchester Primitive Methodist District under the aegis of James Macpherson, a self-educated biblical scholar and linguist, able to read Hebrew, Greek, Latin, German and French. It was the Sunderland District, however, which seized the initiative and gained Conference's approval for the establishment of a theological institute to be housed in the town's former infirmary, built in 1823. Colin M'Kechnie campaigned strongly in favour of John Petty as first Principal but the college committee preferred William Antliff, who took up his duties in July 1868 when 15 students (later increased to 20) were enrolled to launch Primitive Methodism's first genuine theological institution.

Antliff was a member of a Nottinghamshire Primitive Methodist family, which gave three of its sons to the Primitive Methodist ministry – William himself, his brother Samuel, and his son James. All three served as ministers in midland and northern counties, all had scholarly inclinations, and all were in due course awarded honorary Doctorates of Divinity by Methodist universities in North America. James also graduated as M.A. and B.D. as a result of studies at the University of Edinburgh while stationed in that city in the 1870s. All three of them held important Connexional posts, in James Antliff's case in Canada, where he ministered from 1878. He was appointed Editor in 1878 and President of the Canadian Primitive Methodist Conference in 1883.

Nevertheless the fact is that the students at the Sunderland college were to be instructed by a principal and a tutor (Revd Thomas Greenfield, who was later to succeed Antliff as Principal), neither of whom had had any formal ministerial training themselves and whose learning was a product largely of their own efforts. Such were the circumstances within Primitive Methodism ministerial education at that time. Antliff was not a specialist scholar but a man of wide reading, with a good memory, a clear mind and a forceful presence. He was the author of a number of occasional pieces and pamphlets, had edited John Walford's large life of Hugh Bourne (1855–7) and published his own biography of Hugh Bourne in 1872. A critically minded student at the Sunderland Institute, John Day Thompson, remembered Antliff more as a preacher and guide than thinker and theologian. His memory of Thomas Greenfield was warmer:

A scholar to the finger tips, an enthusiastic student of the Bible in the original tongues; a Puritan but also an evangelical theologian of a sturdy type; a most arresting and enlightening expositor. He had a quaint and caustic humour which both endeared and incited.

He was in John Day Thompson's phrase 'anything but a ranter'.

Some 300 students passed through the Sunderland Institute during its lifespan of 1868 to 1882. At a period when the total number of active ministers in the Primitive Methodist Connexion was approximately one thousand, these college-trained men were a considerable element within the whole, representing the results of a college training, limited though it was. Antliff and Greenfield were very much aware of these limitations and must have been severely frustrated by the constraints within which they had to work, not least the meagre educational attainments of a good proportion of the men whom they were accepting for training. Within a 12-month course they could lay a foundation only, and hope that their students would be inspired to enlarge their learning by their own efforts in the course of their ministry. Two notable examples of this come from the very first student entry. Edwin Dalton was to become the Connexional Book Steward and President of the Primitive Methodist Conference and receive a doctorate; and George Parkin was to gain the degrees of M.A. and B.D. from Glasgow University and become the fourth Principal of the Manchester Primitive Methodist College, to whose origins we now turn [38].

The Sunderland Institute had proved both the value of a theological college and the disadvantages of housing it in a second-hand building designed for a quite different purpose. By the mid-1870s ministerial training was rising high in the agenda of Connexional policy, and a decision was taken in 1875 that the time had arrived when a second college was needed, and that it ought to be in Manchester. One of the prime movers in this was James Travis, and it was his zeal and administrative

38. LINES ADDRESSED TO A YOUNG MAN ON LEAVING HOME FOR THE PRIMITIVE METHODIST THEOLOGICAL INSTITUTE, SUNDERLAND.

I

From lovely scenes to thee endeared,
From friends whose smiles have often cheered,
Thou now art going far away,
In the bright morn of op'ning day !

II

Flushed with the hopes of buoyant youth,
Go thou, dear friend, in search of Truth;
At early morn and in thy morn of life,
Gain knowledge, for the coming strife.

III

Great lessons learn beyond compute,
Within our noble Institute;
Then taking helmet, shield and sword,
Rush to the battle of our Lord !

IV

Heroic stand in Jesus' name,
A Saviour's love aloud proclaim, —
Until the glad command is given,
To quit the field, and rest in heaven.

Source: *Flowers in Heaven and other poems*, London 1871, by Lowther E. Ellis (1839–1916), (Primitive Methodist minister).

skills which gave momentum to the whole process. Unfortunately much of the responsibility of realizing the scheme fell to James Macpherson, who had been chosen as Principal-elect but proved woefully inadequate in practical matters and the handling of money. A plot of land on the corner of Alexandra Road South and Gowan Road was eventually acquired and plans drawn for a college to house 30 students. The foundation stones of the new Institute were laid on 24 June 1878 and by the end of 1879 Macpherson was able to take up residence in the Principal's house. The college block, which was the first purpose-built residential educational establishment belonging to the Connexion, was also ready to receive its first intake of students, but it was not to be. Owing to a period of economic depression many Primitive Methodist circuits were short of money and were making do with fewer ministers. The Sunderland College could supply the number needed and rebuffed any idea of sharing students with Manchester, where the college had to be moth-balled for 18 months, finally receiving its first intake of students in July 1881. It was becoming very obvious that the Connexion could not by any means justify two theological colleges, and despite a passionate debate at Conference, held at South Shields in 1883, the Sunderland College was closed. The decision was a bitter blow to Sunderland, and the Primitive Methodist district of which it was the heart, because of its impressive endeavours to promote educational provision for ministers and local preachers over several decades. But it was the correct decision for the future because the new college in Manchester, in due course to take the name of Hartley College, was purpose-built, had the necessary facilities for future growth in ministerial training, and was well placed to exploit the educational potential of relations with Owens College, the University to be.[17] The story of Hartley College is continued in a later chapter.

For discussion

1. Despite modern educational opportunities can Methodist folk still learn lessons of self-improvement from the examples of the early Primitive Methodists?

2. In the light of Primitive Methodism's enthusiasm for mission can you imagine new evangelical ventures open to the Methodist Church of today?

3. Consider the character of Methodist ministerial training today in the light of earlier practice. Your minister could supply useful thoughts on this.

5

Tensions and Progress

As the Primitive Methodist Connexion moved into what might be called its middle age, the period from 1850 to 1890, its more thoughtful ministers and members could not help realizing that while the Connexion could take pride in its many achievements it was increasingly obliged to face up to questionings and tensions which were arising out of its very progress and success. At the heart of these tensions was a complex of developments which were disturbing the relationship between ministers and laity, but had wider ramifications springing from the increasing complexity and modernization of Primitive Methodism in the Victorian period. Some of these issues have already been alluded to in relation to education and ministerial training, but now need to be seen in a wider setting.

Ministerial influence

In 1843 Primitive Methodism's connexional headquarters were transferred to London, with the inevitable development of a centralized administrative system based in the capital, which to some minds represented a challenge to the localized decision-making of circuits and districts. This process was accentuated by the reduction of the independence of Primitive Methodist districts in 1878, especially with regard to ministerial stationing but having wider implications also. Within the districts themselves the later nineteenth century saw a great increase in the number of circuits, by a steady process of subdivision. More circuits meant more ministers on the ground, including a proportionate increase in the number of superintendents, with their greater status and higher wages. Ministerial wages in general were increasing during the period in question, and circuits had other charges to meet in connection with the provision of manses, ministerial training, and above all with the campaign to build new and better chapels which was seen by some of the laity to be largely inspired by ministers. Ministers may well have been in the forefront of the building campaign of the Victorian period out of keenness to provide chapels which could match those of the older Free Church denominations and reflect more adequately the considerable achievements and rising status of Primitive Methodism. There is no doubt that many responsible lay leaders agreed with this policy, but the rank and file may not always have appreciated the loss of their old familiar Bethels in down-town situations and their replacement by expensive new buildings on more favoured sites. It was possible to interpret these developments as a desertion by official Primitive Methodism of its working-class roots in a search for more respectability. It can equally be seen as a natural tendency to keep pace with the attitudes and requirements of much of its membership. There was the source of real dissension here, and the Connexion's ministers were at the centre of it, not necessarily by choice but as a result of trends with which in general they approved, and were the beneficiaries of. Because of the reticence of the Connexional historians to acknowledge openly the sharpness of feeling which these developments generated it is not easy to sense the true nature of

Primitive Methodism at that period and the acute tensions which it was experiencing, while outwardly presenting a picture of impressive progress and enhanced respectability.

Significant evidence for the divided inner state of Primitive Methodism comes from the north east of England, and in particular the Sunderland Primitive Methodist Circuit, where in the later 1870s a deep and serious rift occurred.[1] Outwardly all seemed well. Sunderland Primitive Methodism had a notable history. It had been a Circuit town since 1823 and when the circuits within the Connexion were gathered into four districts in 1824, Sunderland became the centre of the great northern district which at that time stretched from Whitby to Berwick, and west to Carlisle. Sunderland had been the meeting place of the annual Primitive Methodist Conference on four occasions up to the 1860s, and from that date had become the location of Primitive Methodism's first genuine theological college. Primitive Methodism on Wearside was vigorous, appealing strongly to coal miners, shipyard workers, potters and artisans of various trades, and enlisting many of them into responsible roles within its circuit life, as local preachers, class leaders, stewards and teachers in the Sunday schools for both adults and children. A few members were of some substance but Primitive Methodism in Sunderland was from its origins strongly proletarian in character, and its central chapel, built in 1824 on Flag Lane, was situated in a narrow court off the town's ancient High Street, in the very heart of the working-class community of Wearside. Other chapels in more salubrious locations were to be built later but Flag Lane retained the affections of many, and symbolized to them Primitive Methodism's character as the people's church, representing the revivalism out of which Primitive Methodism had grown and which (they hoped) might be born again.

American evangelists such as Walter and Phoebe Palmer in the early 1860s, and Dwight L. Moody and Ira D. Sankey a decade later, were making extended revivalist tours of British towns, Sunderland included, and stirring hopes and dreams of a new age of revival in Britain itself.[2] In the pit villages

which were on Sunderland's doorstep a wave of revivalism did in fact break out in the 1860s and 1870s, largely led by lay evangelists, both men and women. In the town itself William Gelley, a talented evangelist who had been converted by the Palmers, was engaged by the Primitive Methodist circuit to work as a town missionary from 1870. Despite these endeavours, and perhaps provoked by them, there was a growing body of feeling among the Primitive Methodist laity in Sunderland that the Connexion had lost its way and needed to rediscover its mission. There was in particular a growing mood of dissatisfaction with the Connexion's ministers that might almost be described as anti-clericalism, and bitter words were spoken.

Troubles in Sunderland and the Lay Church Secession

The opening of a chapel on Tatham Street in 1875 and the proposed division of the Sunderland Primitive Methodist circuit brought matters to a head. The new chapel was little more than half a mile from Flag Lane but its bourgeois setting within the 'new town' of Bishopwearmouth contrasted markedly with the context of the Flag Lane chapel in the heart of old Sunderland. The new chapel prospered but a proposal to create a new circuit of which it would be the head was strongly resisted by a two-thirds majority of the circuit's leading officials. A high-powered delegation consisting of members of the Primitive Methodist General Committee then visited Sunderland and heard the objections, but on returning to London swept them aside and recommended that the circuit should be divided because of the apparently irreparable rifts within it. The delegation had somewhat desperately hoped to promote peace, but unleashed a whirlwind. The bitterness of feeling in the circuit is best illustrated by letters written to the *Sunderland Daily Echo* by deeply offended lay leaders.[3]

A more tyrannically despotic act never proceeded from any church meeting . . . Shall we suffer the priests to eat out the very heart of the Connexion ... Can we sit down tamely under an act of arbitrary despotism? Shall the character of our connexion be changed by a number of priests and their miserable weaklings?

The inflamed language even now comes as a severe shock, and was continued in letters of a year later, when after various manoeuvrings, the division of the circuit was confirmed:

All confidence is at an end ... This division has been effected by a Conference clique infatuated by a love of power characteristic of the whole priestly hierarchy. They seek not the chief good but little circuits and large salaries. If Primitive Methodism is to be maintained in its original simplicity and power the lay preachers must organize themselves throughout the Connexion and by means of associations of this kind they may be able to arrest the progress of priestly power.

This line of thought is continued more soberly and sadly by one of the Primitive Methodist circuit's leading laymen:

I think it is high time that the laymen of the Primitive Methodist Connexion were astir, and looked about for help somewhere else. It seems obvious that the lay element has no place in the estimation of these gentlemen.

The outcome of this dramatic and bitter episode was that in February 1877 over 300 members of the old Sunderland Primitive Methodist circuit withdrew from Primitive Methodism to form new congregations, served by lay ministers, selected and appointed by the seceders. A preaching plan of the Christian Lay Churches, Sunderland Circuit, was published immediately, with a list of 18 preachers and seven meeting places including a workmen's hall, a shipwrights' hall and rooms in two collieries. Obviously many of the seceders were working-class folk, but there were some prosperous businessmen among

them. They included William Branfoot (1825–1902) whose father John (1795–1831) was one of the very first Primitive Methodist travelling preachers to mission Sunderland (in 1821) and was later to be killed by an accident when walking to a preaching appointment along a local colliery railway. Within the Primitive Methodist community of Sunderland the seceders were (and sometimes still are) referred to as the 'Runaway Ranters'. However, the Lay Church folk themselves felt that it was not they who had deserted Primitive Methodism, but rather that they were recovering its authentic character which official Primitive Methodism itself was in danger of losing, if it was not already lost [39].

The Lay Church secession, and the campaign which preceded it, obviously touched a deep and sensitive nerve within the Primitive Methodist connexion. Its leaders stirred vivid memories of the movement's heroic age, when missionary ventures into ever widening territories were the very essence of

39. We would not have it supposed that in leaving the Connexion with which many of us have been identified since childhood, we have changed our religious views. All that was dear to us in respect of doctrine, or cherished association, is dear to us still, but Primitive Methodism in regard to its polity and the relationship subsisting between its paid ministers and the lay agency and members, is no longer what it once was. As we hold that any departure from the simplicity of the New Testament is fraught with danger, and as we have long perceived a growing tendency to establish a hierarchy in the Church of our fathers, and that widespread dissatisfaction towards this bane of the dissenting Protestant Church is being manifested throughout Christian England, we have resolved to return to the primitive usages laid down in the New Testament believing that a hired ministry is by no means essential.

Source: From the first printed plan published by the Christian Lay Churches in Sunderland in February 1877, following the secession from Primitive Methodism. See *Proceedings of the Wesley Historical Society*, June 1976, p. 138.

the movement. In those remarkable campaigns evangelistic preaching and the winning of converts were the *raison d'être* of Primitive Methodism. Inevitably the competence of a travelling preacher was judged by his success in this enterprise, to which many lay preachers were also committed, working side by side with their full-time, paid brethren. Two generations later all was changed. Revivalism might break out sporadically where a charismatic minister could light the flame, but a minister's work was no longer justified by the number of souls he was converting. The Primitive Methodist ministry was becoming a profession – trained, better paid and better housed, working in compact circuits, and engaged largely in the pastoral care and instruction of a settled congregation housed in pleasant and well-built chapels. The former Ranters had become an established and respected element in the ecclesiastical life of later Victorian England. Yet the troubles in Sunderland in the 1870s showed that the old embers could still be stirred into life, and that many responsible and committed Primitive Methodists could be roused to such a strong sense of unrest with regard to developments within the Connexion as to sever their lifelong commitment to it and opt for a Lay Church. Further research into other areas of the country needs to be done in order to investigate whether or not the troubles in Sunderland were replicated elsewhere. Despite the fact that Sunderland, especially in the old heart of the town, was an outspoken, frank and democratic community, it is hard to think that this can be the only explanation for the reaction there to Primitive Methodist developments which were common to many other areas [40].

As a footnote to the story of the Christian Lay Churches it is interesting to compare it to the secessions from Wesleyan Methodism in the 1820s and 1830s producing the Protestant Methodists and the Wesleyan Methodist Association. The circumstances and conflicts leading to these developments were very similar to those giving rise to the episode in Sunderland Primitive Methodism. Yet the Wesleyan seceders all retained a professional ministry, no doubt because they held a higher view of the min-

---

40. The value of local preachers

Our numbers increase, and we have opened several fresh places during the winter, such as Crewe Lane, Haslington, Wantaley, Wheelock Heath, and other places round about. In this mission work several of the local preachers took an active part. In ability to preach, visit the people and push on the work some of the local preachers were quite equal to the regular ministers, and they had some privileges which the ministers had not. They were becoming widely known, and respected among various classes of society. Hence they were often invited to go and preach at respectable houses to respectable congregations; this often opened the way for establishing regular preaching in various places where societies were soon formed and the cause permanently established.

Source: Thomas Bateman, 'Reminiscences of early Primitive Methodism', *Primitive Methodist Magazine*, 1883, pp. 597–8.

---

istry than did the Sunderland Primitive Methodist seceders, for whom the step towards a lay church was more easily taken.

H. B. Kendall was stationed in Sunderland in the early 1870s and in circuits near to it when the Lay Church secession took place. Yet his account of the episode in his history of the Primitive Methodist Church is brief and enigmatic. He does admit, however, that mistakes were made by the Primitive Methodist authorities, and affirms the central importance of the democratic principle in the Connexion's life and work.[4]

Chapel building and finance

The chapel on Tatham Street, Sunderland, the building of which was one of the causes of grievance in the troubles recounted above, may be used as an example of the great chapel building campaign launched within Primitive Methodism in the Victorian period, especially in its middle and later decades.

Built in red brick, with stone dressings of a Gothic character and with Sunday schools and a manse adjoining, it was the largest chapel built by the Primitive Methodists in the town by that date, and, at £9,000 (about one million pounds in current values), the most expensive. By the mid-1840s the Connexion had 1,300 purpose-built chapels; it proceeded to build something approaching that number in each decade thereafter, up to the end of the century. The impulses driving this impressive building campaign were varied. The numerical growth and geographical expansion of the Connexion, the increasing subdivision of circuits, the rapid expansion of urban communities, and a desire for more commodious and attractive places of worship, all played their part [41]. The enthusiasm of ministers also has to be taken into account.

---

41. Forward movement in Southsea

For nearly a quarter of a century our beloved Church made little, if any, appreciable progress in this fashionable and rapidly advancing part of Portsmouth. It was contented with one church in Somers Road and a small brick building in Albert Road for many years. Eventually a new iron church was erected in front of the small brick building, which had been purchased several years before from the Bible Christians. It was thought if Primitive Methodism were to make anything like the progress it had made in other towns it must enter upon a new regime. Sanction was therefore sought through the proper Connexional courts for Albert Road society in Southsea to be made into a separate circuit or rather pastorate . . . Plans were obtained for two handsome shops, schoolroom, vestries, &c., and a large hall in the amphitheatre style, with semi-circular seats, at a cost, including the value of the land, of nearly £3,500 . . . A new mission is contemplated almost immediately in a rapidly-growing suburb of Southsea, where there is almost a new township of 10,000 people with very little religious accommodation, and no Primitive Methodist church within a mile and a half or two miles.

Source: *Primitive Methodist Magazine*, 1903, pp. 61–3.

The chapel building era developed here and there a minister of a special type . . . The biographies and obituary notices of the time witness to the current belief that some degree of such work as this would come in the way of a minister's regular duty, and must not be shirked; hence next to having had no decrease on his stations, it counted to him as a distinction that he has built or enlarged so many chapels.[5]

The founder of the campaign of chapel extension (insofar as one man can be singled out in this respect) was John Bywater (1804–69), a Leeds man who served as a Primitive Methodist minister for 37 years, 14 of them in the Hull Circuit.[6] He was largely responsible for the chapel on Great Thornton Street, and the Clowes Chapel, Jarratt Street, both in Hull and particularly impressive examples of the style that was to be much copied later. Bywater made a beginning and others followed his example. 'It was impossible afterwards to build a paltry chapel or to be satisfied with an obscure situation. The offshoots of Great Thornton Street and Jarratt Street claimed the right to come to the front and to the front they came.' Nor was the influence limited to Hull. It went into all the circuits in the Hull District which became famous in the Connexion for its magnificent chapels.

Despite the ravages of urban renewal and the closure and demolition of many chapels, examples of this remarkable chapel building campaign of the Primitive Methodists can still be found here and there. Those readers with access to H. B. Kendall's *History of the Primitive Methodist Church* can browse through the pages towards the end of volume 2 where the fruits of the great building campaign can be seen in page after page of photographic displays of chapels in the major urban communities where Primitive Methodism was strong – Leicester, Hull, Sunderland, Nottingham, Luton, Derby, Birmingham, Bradford, Middlesbrough, Manchester, Gateshead and Darlington, with many individual photographs along the way. The buildings overall are impressive in size and character, with the predominant architectural styling and decoration usually confined to the public 'face' and entrance. The style of many of these chapels is not easy to determine or describe; it has to be described as a kind of debased 'classical' architecture, with a large triangular pediment over the main front as the distinctive feature, as used by Bywater on Jarratt Street, Hull. The convenience of this style was that it could be used in a varying scale from simplicity to grandeur, according to the money available. Some buildings in this same style were given Gothic rather than classical detail, and occasionally there was a much more wholehearted use of the Gothic style, as at Higher Ardwick in Manchester with its impressive spire. It has to be admitted that some Primitive Methodist chapels were indeterminate in their character and a few were distinctly odd.

In the 1870s, 879 Primitive Methodist chapels were built at an average individual cost of £1,179, and a total cost of £1,057,511. These figures have to be multiplied by around one hundred times to indicate current values today. There was of course a tremendous range in the costs involved, related to the size and quality of the buildings themselves. Tatham Street chapel in Sunderland at £9,000 was one of the more expensive chapels of that period, but was greatly exceeded by Higher Ardwick chapel in Manchester which cost £15,000. This last sum was to be exceeded by the 'Central' Primitive Methodist church built on Northumberland Road, Newcastle in 1899 to replace the venerable old chapel on Nelson Street. Central was the fruit of the inspiration and labours of its minister, Revd Arthur T. Guttery, D.D., who had an unusually long ministry in Newcastle from 1895 to 1908. It cost £16,000 and was stone built with a Gothic exterior and spire, but its handsome and spacious worship area with its large gallery was essentially a preaching room in which Gothic detail (including some stained glass windows) played a minor role. What must have been the most expensive chapel built in the name of Primitive Methodism was opened on Church Street, Southport, in 1906. Now known as St Mark's, it cost £25,000, a large part of which was donated by Sir William Hartley, the Primitive Methodist jam-maker

and philanthropist who features later in these pages. It is Gothic in style, with a dominant tower and spire, a 'church' interior with chancel, fine woodwork and stained glass windows in memory of Sir William and Lady Hartley given by their daughters.[7] Another church of a similar size and style was built nearby at St Anne's on Sea, at about the same date as St Mark's. Both were the product of an initiative (it was even referred to as a mission) to cater for Primitive Methodists who had prospered in business in the Yorkshire and Lancashire mill towns and retired to this 'English Riviera'. It is all a clear sign of Primitive Methodism's tendency, one might even say duty, to cater for increasingly respectable tastes within its own membership.

Travellers who enjoy seeking out old chapels on their tours and have an interest in the buildings of Primitive Methodism are recommended to visit Hexham. The town and its abbey, with the seventh-century crypt built by St Wilfrid as part of his monastic church, are well known. Less familiar are three surviving chapels built by the Primitive Methodists over a period of 80 years and in their varied size and architecture reflecting the character and development of Primitive Methodism throughout that period. The first was a plain building on Bull Bank, partly paid for by Squire Robert Ingram Shafto of Bavington, and opened in 1830 when the preacher was the hymn writer William Sanders, Hugh Bourne's friend and colleague. It cost £800. In 1863 a new chapel on Back Lane (St Mary's Chare), Hexham, was opened in memory of the Primitive Methodist travelling preacher Henry Hebbron, costing £1,400. And finally, owing to the leadership of the Revd John G. Bowran (known widely by his pen-name Ramsey Guthrie), the impressive Central Church was opened in 1909, costing £6,000. The church is large, stone built, in a prominent position in the town centre, and dramatic in its character and style which is essentially Gothic but (to quote Professor Pevsner) of a 'fanciful style'. Its interior was noted for its splendid oak panelling. All three chapels are no longer in use for Methodist worship, but to ponder their exteriors with understanding and a little historical knowledge can help to bring to life the nature of the movement which they represent.

As chapels increased in size and refinement the employment of professional architects became a necessity, as was the case with the Central Chapel, Hexham, for which a well-known Newcastle firm was engaged. Certain architects who had a personal allegiance to Primitive Methodism found themselves so busily engaged in designing chapels for the Connexion, that it became their particular specialism. Two fine examples from the north east were George Race (a Weardale man) and T. E. Davidson, both of whom had a particular sensitivity to the requirements of Primitive Methodist Chapels and Sunday schools, and designed some very satisfying examples, combining practicality and simplicity with a pleasing aesthetic sense. A similar role was played in the West Riding and Lancashire by Thomas Howdill (1840–1918), originally from Tadcaster, but later based in Leeds. Originally a joiner, he developed an increasingly successful architectural practice in which his son Charles became a partner in 1893.

Cultural progress

The fuller development of scholarship and culture within Primitive Methodism is a significant aspect of the Connexion's character in the later nineteenth century. How fully this movement influenced the rank and file of the Connexion's members is a question impossible to answer. It is very likely that a good proportion ignored it and some may even have derided it. Yet it certainly had a wide influence in the Connexion, and those who did not themselves have an active share in it could recognize its worth and importance and encourage within their children the value of education and self-culture [42].

Ministers had a key role in the dissemination of these attitudes, to which their own improved training was a valuable incentive. The more thoughtful local preachers, Sunday school teachers and class leaders also had much influence, though it is difficult today to find surviving evidence of it. What can be assessed

42. If some of the holy and honoured men who accomplished such wonders during the Connexion's infancy were still living amongst us, with the acquirements they then possessed, would their zeal and piety atone for their lack of education? Would our intelligent friends [i.e. adherents] willingly sit under their ministry? Do not our people generally require something for thought? . . . [Unless we meet this challenge] we shall have the mortification of seeing the intelligent part of our people, the young especially, deserting our ministry for one of higher attainments, and better qualified to teach!

Source: *Primitive Methodist Magazine*, 1864, p. 466 (paraphrased).

is the content of the Connexion's more solid regular publications, especially the monthly magazine and the quarterly *Christian Ambassador*, later taking the name of the *Primitive Methodist Quarterly Review*, and later still the *Holborn Review*. The prime aim of the monthly magazine was to promote a strong awareness of the connexional character of Primitive Methodism. The mid-century issues were filled with profuse accounts of chapel openings and anniversaries, of endless tea meetings, of biographical sketches and obituaries of ministers and lay leaders, of illustrations of religious progress and revivals, all stressing the working of providence within the Connexion. Poetry began to be given a noticeable presence in the *Magazine* by 1860 but it was in the later decades of the century, under James Macpherson and Colin Campbell M'Kechnie as editors, that real changes were introduced, in the shape of solid theological instruction, and the introduction of serious and well-researched items on history, biography, literature, politics, current affairs and natural history, the last of these being much enriched by the regular contributions of the Revd Alfred Campbell (1858–1931), Fellow of the Linnaean Society. To attract family reading of the magazine, serialized novels were introduced, on homely themes. To take one example, the bound volume of the *Magazine* for 1900, by then bearing the title *Aldersgate*, contains (among much else) a ladies' page, descriptive accounts (with photographs) of the New Forest and the Eden valley, items on Christian Science and London street lore, a serialized story by Joseph Hocking, an earnest analysis of the future of Africa, and a carefully considered piece on the development within the Connexion away from large circuits and towards more concentrated pastorates, especially in urban areas.

Readers of a more scholarly cast of mind could turn to the quarterly where the articles were of a serious nature with history, biography, theology, philosophy, literature and contemporary life and religion all represented. The quarterly was one of the finest flowers of the intellectual strand in Primitive Methodism, which itself can be traced back to the influence of Hugh Bourne himself. It is helpful here to illustrate this theme by a specific example, Thomas Shepherd Widdowson (1862–97), the son of a Primitive Methodist itinerant preacher. He trained at Borough Road College, became a London school master, was appointed one of Her Majesty's school inspectors, and became a largely self-made scholar in the fields of history and antiquarianism. When Toynbee Hall opened as a University Settlement in the east end of London he threw in his lot with the work there. He was a book collector and gave lectures, illustrated by his own lantern slides, on serious subjects such as the life of Sir Thomas More. This interesting and talented man sadly died at the age of 35. There are oak doors with copper inscriptions to his memory at Toynbee Hall.[8] Impressive reminders of him are the historical pieces he wrote for the *Primitive Methodist Magazine*. A typical example is a closely researched item on the Anglo-Saxon carved stone cross at Ruthwell in south-western Scotland, illustrated by fine engravings of two faces of the cross, and including within the text of the piece a translation of the ancient poem *The Dream of the Rood*, part of which is carved upon it. The writer here has to acknowledge the value of this piece by Tom Widdowson which providentially came to his notice after having sought for information on the Ruthwell Cross for some time without success.[9]

Sunday schools and the Christian Endeavour

Sunday schools were a feature of Primitive Methodism from its early years and Hugh and James Bourne published a monthly *Children's Magazine* from the press at Bemersley. A copy of the bound volume for 1835 is before me as I write, about the size of a pocket diary, with quaint woodcut illustrations at the head of each monthly issue [43]. The tone of the publication is predictably earnest and the youthful readers are addressed virtually as adults on the serious matters of Christian faith and obedience. There is also a frank acceptance of matters of life and death, including the deaths of children and young people, several of which are recorded at some length in this volume. At the same time Hugh Bourne's practical approach to religion and learning is evident, as in a piece written by him on the teaching of the alphabet to infants. He acknowledges the value of mingling amusement with instruction, and provides a poem on the capital letters which can be recited or even sung by the children, set as he explains to any common metre tune [44].

Such basic instruction implies the inadequacy of secular education at that period, and it was in

---

43. The Lord, by means of Sunday Schools has brought the children into more peculiar [i.e. particular] notice. Thousands of grown up people are usefully employed in this excellent service . . . and many talents brought into action . . . Two hours in the forenoon with an hour and a quarter, or an hour and a half in the afternoon, makes a good Sunday School day . . . Industry and faith in God are the chief things . . . It would be well if all our people were conversant with these blessed institutions which have been one great means of peopling heaven.

Source: A piece written by Hugh Bourne, and dating from early in the Connexion's life. Republished in *The General Consolidated Minutes of the Primitive Methodist Connexion*, 1850.

44. Two feet, one head, and score across,
   In letter A we see
   And one stroke down, and two half-rounds
   Complete the letter B.
   The letter Y stands quite upright,
   And shows its open head,
   And one slant stroke, with head and foot,
   Completes the letter Z.
   The Lord our God on Sinai,
   Did write for us we know;
   Letters he gave, and written laws,
   That we to heaven might go.

Source: 'On the small letters', *Primitive Methodist Children's Magazine*, 1835, pp. 60–1.

Sunday or Evening schools that not only children but also adults gained a basic education which in many cases was the foundation of a process of lifelong learning [45].

By the mid-century the *Primitive Methodist Juvenile Magazine*, which was sold for one penny in monthly issues, offered a mixture of religious and general information and instruction, with fine engravings as illustrations. The tone was evangelical and strict, as would be expected. An article in the *Juvenile Magazine* for 1855 warned strongly of the dangers of reading novels, declaring that 'the popular novels of our day are, to a great extent, written by men who are known to be lax in principle and loose in life'! Even Sir Walter Scott does not escape condemnation. Such narrowness was unduly protective and no doubt many lively-minded young Primitive Methodists could not accept it. Yet it does indicate an anxiety that Sunday schools should be concerned not only with instruction and learning but also with moral discipline and an attachment to the Church. This concern became more acute in the later nineteenth century when, in contrast to the early revivalist period, the membership of the Connexion was sustained more from within its own ranks than from without.

The *Sunday School Report* of 1893 spoke of the Church and the Sunday school as 'essentially one', and described the schools as 'not merely seminaries for teaching but saving agencies'. The idea of a Sunday School Union seems to have originated in the Leeds Circuit, with William Beckworth as one of its founders. The Primitive Methodist Conference adopted the principle for the entire Connexion in 1874, one of the main aims being to weld the schools 'into vital union with the Church'. Thirty years later the Sunday school statistics showed over 4,000 schools, 60,000 teachers, and nearly 470,000 scholars, 76,000 of whom were already members of the Primitive Methodist Church.[10] The General Secretaryship of the Primitive Methodist Sunday Schools was by this date one of the most influential connexional appointments. The Revd George Bennett, who held the post from 1907 until 1912, was described as 'preaching, lecturing and organizing from one end of the denomination to the other' to promote the Sunday school cause.[11] An important achievement of his was to ensure that the Christian Endeavour became an integral part of Primitive Methodist Church life.

The Young People's Society of Christian

45. Sabbath schools are England's glory
   Let them spread on every hand:
   They send forth the Saviour's story
   To the thousands of our land:
   Sabbath scholars should be heedful
   Of the blessings they enjoy:
   God will send them more than needful,
   And will all their wants supply.

   Let the sinner seek his pleasure
   In the wicked ways of sin;
   But give me the richer pleasure
   Of a gospel-hope within:
   This will be more satisfying
   Than the riches of Peru;
   This will bless me when I'm dying,
   More than they can ever do.

Source: W. Antliff, *Primitive Methodist Sabbath School Hymn Book*, 1865, No. 29, vv. 1 and 3.

Endeavour began around 1880 in America as a movement founded by the Revd Dr F. E. Clark, a Congregationalist born in Canada but then working in the USA, to encourage social and educational interests as part of a serious Christian commitment, and was introduced into England in 1896. It was aimed at young people of 14 and over and encouraged their loyalty by the use of a membership card, a badge, and a personal pledge of commitment to the movement and its activities. A regular programme of weekly meetings for fellowship, testimony and prayer was planned and published in advance, one meeting a month being a 'consecration' meeting. The programme of the Endeavour was intended to create a sense of purpose and involvement, and the different members were given tasks to perform according to their age and ability. Each member was appointed to serve in one or more of the movement's sectional committees, among them a Mission Band Committee, a Temperance Committee, the evocatively named Sunshine Committee, and others [46]. By the early 1900s there were 57,000 branches of the Endeavour worldwide and over 3,000 branches in

---

46. Christian Endeavour: Active Member's Pledge.

Relying on the Lord Jesus Christ for salvation, and trusting in God for strength, I promise Him that I will strive to do whatever He would have me to do; I will pray to Him and read the Bible every day, I will support my own Church and its services in every way within my power, and throughout my whole life I will endeavour, by the help of the Holy Spirit, to lead a Christian life. As an Active Member, I promise to be true to all my duties, to be present at, and to take some part other than singing, in every meeting unless hindered by some reason which I can conscientiously give to my Lord and Master Jesus Christ. If obliged to be absent from the monthly consecration meeting, I will, if possible, send the reason for absence to the Society.

Source: *The General Rules of the Primitive Methodist Church Revised*, 1923.

---

47. This new movement, the Christian Endeavour, came into Scotland Gate with William Hartley.* He had a wonderful way with young people of which he was quite unconscious, and he stimulated, encouraged and counselled us and yet enabled us to do things. Before he had been long with us he had started a Christian Endeavour Society and had persuaded the chapel stewards to allot it an evening in the week. He was helped by 'Maggie Jane', a crippled woman who nevertheless had abundant vitality, and by Willie Pattison, a young carpenter and undertaker. Those three were an admirable combination and before long the Endeavour was the strongest society connected with the chapel. Somebody had the bright idea of giving it the status of a class meeting and all members of the Endeavour who were also members of the chapel were deemed to be on the books of this particular 'class'. We met in the schoolroom, on the wall of which was now displayed a large copy of the Y.P.S.C.E. pledge. We used the hymns of Ira D. Sankey, and by ordering them in bulk we were able to have the name of our own society printed diagonally across the cover. Committees were set up and I found myself a member of the Sunshine Committee. Thereby I learned to sing hymns unaccompanied in other people's houses and so lost a good deal of the self-consciousness which was my chief affliction.

Source: A. Victor Murray, *A Northumbrian Methodist Childhood*, p. 82. Murray is writing here of the first decades of the twentieth century.

* Not to be confused with W. P. Hartley, the Primitive Methodist jam manufacturer.

England, based in a variety of nonconformist churches, Baptist, Congregational, United Methodist and Primitive Methodist. The Wesleyans on the whole preferred their equivalent organization, the Wesley Guild. District Unions brought together the various Christian Endeavour Societies in occasional meetings, rallies and outings, where amid a good deal of fun the seeds of an ecumenical outlook might be sown. Through its friendly and communal character the Endeavour was encouraging a sense of the unity of the churches, and of the value of talking and learning and growing in knowledge within the fellowship of chapel life, all related to a steadily maturing faith.

In the Christian progress of young people the Endeavour proved to be a valuable link between Sunday school and church membership. It was also a forum in which a developing Christian commitment could be confirmed [47]. The Revd Dr Robert F. Wearmouth, one of Methodism's most eminent social historians, was converted in a Christian Endeavour mission at the little Primitive Methodist chapel in the mining community of Oxhill, County Durham; and when he progressed to become a theological student at Hartley College he found his devotional life there catered for by a lively Christian Endeavour run by the students [48].

48. As a young person much of the life of the chapel for me centred round Sunday School and the Junior Christian Endeavour. CE was a good training ground for, if you went to a meeting, you were expected to take part, and say something. Victor Murray in his autobiography, implies that the Christian Endeavour took the place of the class meeting for some. It was certainly so for me. I never knew a real class meeting until I became a member of the 'Cambridge Groups' in university. On joining the 'Endeavour' I signed a pledge card: 'Relying on the Lord Jesus Christ for salvation and trusting in God for strength, I promise . . .' among the promises was one that required me to be present at the monthly consecration meeting and every week be prepared to 'take part aside from singing'. Seeking for, and saying, *something* was a good preparation for later preaching.

Source: John Banks, *A Primitive Cradling*, the 7th Englesea Brook Chapel Aid Lecture, 1997.

For discussion

1. Could the related roles of lay folk and ministers in modern Methodism be arranged more fruitfully?

2. Are we making the most of our heritage of older chapels, and are we building new ones which are adapted to modern needs, and likely to satisfy congregations for years to come?

3. Did Primitive Methodism's character and mode of working impose particular, and even undue, pressures upon its ministers?

4. 'Local and lay in its emphasis rather than Connexional and ministerial'. Is this a fair summary of the character of Primitive Methodism?

5. Consider the role played by the Christian Endeavour in local chapel life, either from personal experience or the memories of others. Is there still a role for this kind of learning and informed discussion in chapel life?

6

Social Influence

The Primitive Methodist Connexion came into being not to bring about social change but to save souls. As history shows time and again, however, a secondary social effect is an almost inevitable consequence of a primary evangelical cause. The working out of this process is a complex interaction of religious experience and human behaviour, of the mutual working of heart and mind and will, under the impulse of a powerful response to the gospel and a commitment to the Christian way of life as represented by some new movement of reformation and revival. The nature of the religious experience and discipline typical of early Primitive Methodism has been outlined earlier in this book. Here we are concerned with the practical outworking, both personal and communal, of this experience. Some of the results were welcomed by the Primitive Methodist authorities, others were unforeseen and unwelcome.

A heightened sense of self-awareness, of personal responsibility and of self-discipline was at the heart of what we might call the Primitive Methodist experience. The experience itself was communal but had to be lived out personally. It involved commitment to the worship and prayer life of the local worshipping Society, and acceptance of Connexional disciplines. There was in all this a strong impulse towards self-improvement, both morally and in thought, knowledge and demeanour. This motivation was strengthened by the responsibility resulting from appointment to office, as class leader, prayer leader, Sunday school teacher or local preacher. Basic education leading to more advanced studies was implicit in these responsibilities, as were the demands to acquire the confidence and skills necessary to lead others in prayer, to offer guidance in moral and religious matters, and to speak audibly and convincingly in public places, whether in chapel, Sunday school or the open air.

Such experiences led many men and (in the earlier years) some women also to become travelling preachers. Those who retained a lay status could still exercise an extensive ministry within the expansive circuits typical of the early period of the Connexion, and there were ample opportunities for lay evangelical initiatives [49]. We have to imagine working folk preaching and ministering to working folk, and their families, and endeavouring to relate the gospel to the hard realities of the everyday lives of their congregations. In these circumstances, and at that particular period, it is not surprising that some Primitive Methodists should become engaged with the burgeoning trade unions.

Trade Unionism

The Durham coalfield produced an early and particularly interesting example in the person of Tommy Hepburn (1795–1854) who, despite being celebrated on a Post Office stamp in 1976 is not as well known as he deserves to be.[1] Born near Chester le Street, he began work at Fatfield Colliery at the age of 8, and in 1822 threw in his lot with the first Primitive Methodists to evangelize the north east, becoming in due course a class leader and local preacher. Methodism gave a lot to Hepburn – faith and fellow-

49. Scarcely a year has elapsed since our cause was introduced into the northern part of this circuit. And, although the period is short, yet abundant fruit has appeared: a very blessed and glorious work has gone on for some time in Sunderland and the neighbouring collieries. In Sunderland and Monk Wearmouth (which is a village on the opposite side of the river from Sunderland) we have nearly four hundred members. In Lord Stewart's and Esquire Lambton's Collieries we have near four hundred more! Some of the most abandoned characters have tasted that the Lord is gracious. Indeed the Lord and the poor colliers are doing wondrously. Our congregations are immensely large, and well-behaved. It would do any of the lovers of Jesus good to see the dear colliers sometimes under the word. On some occasions, (for want of time to wash themselves,) they are constrained to come "Black" to the preaching or else miss the sermon. And when the Lord warms their hearts with his dying love, and they feel him precious in his word, the large and silent tears rolling down their black cheeks, and leaving the white streaks behind, conspicuously portray what their hearts feel. Their hearty and zealous exertions in the cause of God would make almost any one love them. We have five preachers employed in this circuit, and a blessed prospect. May the Lord so continue his work that the 'North may completely give up, and the south keep not back,' until the ends of the earth are converted to the Lord. Isa. xliii.6.

Source: N. West, *Primitive Methodist Magazine*, 1824, pp. 10–11.

ship, moral values, the incentive and opportunity to advance his education, and a context in which to develop his skills as a public speaker (indoors and in the open air) and as a leader of men.

Primitive Methodism's official policy at this time was to discourage active involvement in politics and trade unionism, though the latter was legalized by 1825. Anxiety over threats to the miners' pay and security led to a strike in the north-eastern coalfield in 1831 and the emergence of a miners' trade union, of which Hepburn was the leading spirit. Open-air demonstrations, notable for the control and discipline of the great crowds involved, took place under Hepburn's leadership. A contemporary cartoon shows him on one of these occasions, attempting to negotiate with the coal owners, dressed very respectably in frock coat and top hat and standing under a banner proclaiming 'Patience and Perseverance will recover our Rights'. Some concessions were briefly won, but in the end the union was broken and Hepburn unjustly discredited. Some condemned him for being a dangerous radical, others for not being radical enough. Primitive Methodism felt obliged to disown him.

Some of the chief collieries affected by the strike were within the Sunderland Primitive Methodist Circuit of which John Petty was then the superintendent. His diary entries in the summer of 1832 show a profound concern for the disruptive consequences of the strike and especially its effects on the work of Primitive Methodism.[2] He makes no mention of Hepburn, and expresses no sympathy or concern for the miners' cause. Petty was by no means a hard-hearted minister; he was simply responding to the evangelical priorities of his time. The day of the 'Social Gospel' had not yet arrived. But the seeds were sown for the growth of new attitudes as the century advanced, and for the emergence of a distinguished cadre of Methodist Trade Union leaders who were to be fully and gratefully acknowledged for their contribution to the health and stability of Victorian society.

The chief Primitive Methodist representatives of this group were farmworkers or coal miners. Joseph Arch (1826–1919), a Warwickshire man, left school at 9 to become a bird-scarer and ploughboy, eventually earning a good wage as an expert hedge cutter.[3] Primitive Methodism engaged his loyalty as a young man and he cut his teeth as an orator in his work as a local preacher. His active commitment to Primitive Methodism was not prolonged but skills in speaking, leadership and the organization of men, so vital to early unionism, had been acquired. Primitive Methodism's close-knit network of meetings at various levels from the local to the national must also have offered a model of how a large and widespread organization such as a trade union might be effectively structured [50]. The National Agricultural Labourers' Union which he was largely instrumental in launching in 1872 had, within two years, almost 100,000 members and a thousand branches. The role of Primitive Methodism in these developments was publicly acknowledged and appreciated by important public figures such as Bishop James Fraser of Manchester and Cardinal Manning. The social historian and Member of Parliament, James Thorold

---

50. The interplay and interweaving of religious emotions, ideals, and language in Trade Unionism may perhaps be explained in two ways. Many Trade Union leaders were evangelists and local preachers, fervent members for the most part of Methodist congregations. They had learned to exercise impassioned and persuasive speech in their prayers and sermons and they had acquired knowledge of crusading and of organizing in the chapels and circuits to which they belonged.

On the other hand the early Trade Unionists desired to see religion as an ally; at the century's beginning the Unions were banned, after 1825 permissible, in the second half of the century firmly rooted. The first fifty years were troubled and clouded with a series of defeats and disappointments; almost everywhere magistrates, masters, military, Ministers of State, were in battle-array against the pioneers whose most earnest efforts and importunity only served, it seemed, to goad the opposition to sterner acts of oppression and severer processes of suppression. It was natural, therefore, for the working classes to turn to the Bible and to religion, finding there both bread and light to sustain and guide their spirits and uphold and illuminate their faith. They were struggling against principalities and powers; they were passing through the wilderness and the story of Israel came close to their pulses; they were suffering persecutions and the words of the Old Testament prophets sounded with intimate emphases. The God of justice must be on their side, they felt, and what was more the New Testament fed them as with the manna of hope.

Source: R. F. Wearmouth, *Some Working Class Movements of the 19th Century*, 1948, pp. 320–1.

Rogers, commented that 'Primitive Methodism had done more with limited means for labourers in the countryside than any other religious agency'. The career of George Edwards (1850–1933) is neatly summed up in the title of his autobiography *From Crow Scaring to Westminster* (1922). He was a deeply committed Primitive Methodist, a delegate to the Trades Union Congress, and active in the Eastern Counties Agricultural Labourers' Union. 'His work for the agricultural labourers of East Anglia is a worthy sequel and supplement to that of Joseph Arch in Warwickshire'.[4] In 1906 he founded the National Allied and Agricultural Workers Union, and in 1920 (having switched his political allegiance from Liberal to Labour) he was elected M.P. for South Norfolk.

What might be called 'the Tommy Hepburn tradition' of active Primitive Methodist involvement in the social and political life of the coal miners of the north east coalfield was impressively continued by some distinguished examples in the later nineteenth and early twentieth centuries. Two of them, John Wilson and Thomas Burt, were both born in 1837, and Peter Lee a generation later in 1864.[5] Wilson and Burt enjoyed similar careers south and north of the river Tyne. Both were employed as miners from an early age, both were active in the formation and running of their respective county miners' associations, both became Liberal Members of Parliament, and both were associated with Primitive Methodism, closely in Wilson's case. Burt's parents were Primitive Methodists; though never a member himself, he contributed articles to the *Primitive Methodist Quarterly Review* including one on 'Methodism and the Northern Miners'.[6] Peter Lee's roving career has something about it of his gypsy ancestry, but he settled down in his later twenties, after working as a miner in various parts of England, and in South Africa and the USA. Conversion, a commitment to Primitive Methodism, work as a local preacher, and a serious effort to develop his education stabilized his life and set him on course to become General Secretary of the Durham Miners' Association and President of the national Mineworkers' Federation in 1932. He became a highly effective Chairman of the Durham County Council in 1919, and the regard in which he was held is indicated by the naming of Peterlee new town in County Durham after him [51].

The Primitive Methodist miners' leaders were respected in Parliament. The Clerk of the House of Commons, Erskine May, said of John Wilson's maiden speech, 'Wilson is the most eloquent man who has come into the House this Session. He must be a local preacher!' But the real political and social influence of these men was wielded through the Miners' Associations of their respective districts. Wilson's concern for the miners' welfare led him to become an active promoter of the scheme to provide Aged Miners' Homes. But like Thomas Burt, he remained staunchly loyal to the Liberal Party even after the miners' unions had affiliated with the Labour Party in 1909. It was Wilson's personality and authority that kept Liberalism alive in Durham up to the year of his death in 1915.

Behind the high-profile Methodist leaders there were many mineworkers who endeavoured to keep true to Christian loyalties and standards, and to witness to their faith within the colliery community and in the dark and dangerous circumstances of work down the pit. A multitude of incidents of such behaviour have inevitably disappeared unrecorded, but here and there is a revealing flash of light. A dramatic example is to be found in the story of the disaster which occurred at Seaham Colliery, on 8 September 1880, when 164 men and boys perished, many of whom were trapped down the pit and suffered a slow death. When the rescuers finally broke through the blocked shaft they found at the bottom of the pit a poignant message chalked on a wooden plank. It reads as follows: 'The Lord is with us. We are all ready for heaven. Bless the Lord. We have had a jolly prayer meeting, every man ready for glory. Praise the Lord. Signed Ric. Cole'. Richard Cole was a Primitive Methodist local preacher who would often have ministered to his colleagues from the pulpit. Here at the tragic conclusion of his life, and in unimaginable and deeply moving circumstances, he ministered to them for the last time, as a dying man to dying men.[7]

The story of the close relationship between Methodism and working-class movements was voluminously told in a series of books by Robert F. Wearmouth (1882–1963), a Durham miner and Primitive Methodist minister. His works are valuable, with very many brief biographical accounts illuminating his theme, but lack a critical approach. A more rigorous analysis of this same theme was offered in 1974 by the sociologist Robert Moore in his book *Pitmen, Preachers and Politics*.[8] His approach was that of a social investigator of four small Durham mining communities. By winning the trust of the villagers, he and they were enabled to come to a sharper memory and understanding of what had been happening to their villages and to Methodism within their lifetime, and before that by historical delving. While giving credit for what Methodism had given to the pit villages, Moore showed that in the nineteenth and early twentieth centuries it had also become too closely identified with Liberalism and a conciliatory attitude to labour relations, thereby losing the allegiance of the more critical younger Methodists.

---

51. He visioned a socialized world in which human beings were freed from oppressive economic conditions in order to give full expression to personality . . . But the end was not merely social betterment; it was personal freedom, so that men and women released from the thraldom of a mean life materially, should advance to the Kingdom of God where the unlimited resources of the soul find free play and make the world's pleasures seem cheap . . . There was another thing about religion for Peter Lee, and his sermons were saturated with it. We are all members of one body, and men and women have their personal duties to society as well as rights to claim from it. Service, always service, was on his lips, not as a sentiment, but as a fact of life.

Source: Lawson, *Peter Lee*, 1949, p. 142.

Primitive Methodists in business

Owing to its character and situation the substantial village of North Cave, a few miles west of Hull, was soon caught up in William Clowes's first mission into East Yorkshire, early in 1819. A stroller through North Cave some 80 years later would come upon a substantial tailor's shop, under the ownership of a Mr John Sissons. If our stroller were to be invited into the living quarters over the shop he would discover on the walls a portrait of William Clowes and a substantial library of Primitive Methodist literature, clear signs that the owner and his family were staunch Primitive Methodists. John Sissons was one of that considerable number of Primitive Methodists who, like countless other aspiring nonconformists, had ventured into trade or business, in this case that of a tailor. An aunt had enabled him to take his first shop, and a generous Quaker helped him to take, and stock, a better one. I am not aware that John Sissons's business prospered to any unusual extent, though if it had done so he would once again have been typical of other successful nonconformist entrepreneurs who, starting from small beginnings, showed a strong business acumen, and flourished in their undertakings.[9]

Just as an active commitment to Primitive Methodism led many men into Unionism, it led many others into taking a shop. The appeal of the latter presumably was public usefulness, contact with people, and the independence of running a private concern. Hugh and James Bourne had virtually financed Primitive Methodism in its beginning out of the income from their farming and timber business, and they had many followers within the Connexion who not only supported themselves from their commercial activities but were able to donate some of their wealth to Primitive Methodism. It has to be admitted that such giving was not unduly generous throughout much of the nineteenth century. The main reasons probably were the relative weakness of connexionalism within Primitive Methodism, and the unwillingness of some nouveaux riches to part with their hard-won gains. In any case it was well into the nineteenth century before the proportion of well-to-do members had acquired any real significance. A sample survey of Methodist-owned businesses in the north east of England over the period c.1760–1920 showed that, out of a total of 65, 45 were run by Wesleyan owners, and only 9 by Primitive Methodists. The survey admittedly was partial but the proportions are significant.[10]

The profits (where known) from these Primitive Methodist businesses, as revealed by their owners' wills, varied widely. George Race (1810–86), a Weardale grocer and draper, left £1,400; John Gordon Black (1791–1851), a Sunderland lime manufacturer, left £7,000; Henry Hodge (1812–89), an oilcake manufacturer of Hull, left £62,000; and John Clapham (1847–1923) of Yarm on Tees, the owner of a ropery, left over a quarter of a million pounds though this was largely the result of a commercial interest in shipping. Among this number the Meek family of York deserve a mention. James Meek senior (1790–1862), a York alderman and a Wesleyan Methodist, left £60,000 from his profits as currier and glass maker, and was chairman of two railways. His son James (1815–91) left the Wesleyans to throw in his lot with Primitive Methodism. He held the York mayoralty three times, as well as serving as Deputy Lieutenant of the North Riding. He is said to have been the first Primitive Methodist to receive a knighthood, awarded to him in 1869 after entertaining the Prince of Wales in York during his period as Lord Mayor. Probably because of his social commitments, as well as generous donations to Elmfield College and the Sunderland Theological Institution, James Meek junior left only £16,000 in his will. Another Primitive Methodist who received a knighthood was the Lincolnshire boot factor James Blindell (1884–1937).[11] His award dated from 1934, after Methodist Union, but was the fruit of his benevolence earlier in his career in founding the Flottergate Benevolent Homes in Grimsby, and his public service in local government and as a Member of Parliament for Holland and Boston. Sir James's career was in the classic mould, from virtual rags to riches. The prosperity of another Grimsby businessman, Henry Smethurst (1819–92), was appropriately built upon the fish trade. Public service and the promotion of temperance were his major social concerns. Thomas Robinson of Cleethorpes (1855–1927) was also the owner of a fishing fleet, and was yet another Primitive Methodist business knight, receiving the award as recognition for his work on behalf of food control in World War I[12] [52]. Such men were typical of many others, to be found especially in midland and northern industrial towns. The most distinguished and influential Primitive Methodist businessman, the Aintree jam-maker Sir William Hartley, merits special notice which is to be found in a later chapter.

---

52. At fourteen Thomas Robinson was a cabin boy on a fishing smack. Within another fourteen years he had passed through every grade of a fisherman's life, from cabin boy to master. As a smack owner he built up a sound business, establishing himself on the fish market as a merchant. He had a fleet of 20 steam trawlers, of which 14 were handed over to the government at the outbreak of war. He also served as advisor to the Board of Fisheries on matters of fish food and fish control. For these services he received the honour of a Knight Commander of the Order of the British Empire. He was a strong supporter of the Primitive Methodist Orphanages and served as the Vice President of the Primitive Methodist Conference 1923.

Source: William Leary, *Some Lincolnshire Methodists*, 1998, pp. 46–8.

Temperance

The Primitive Methodist Connexion was not teetotal from its origins. In that early period there must have been a fairly general acceptance of beer and ale for personal consumption, and the provision of wine, or some other beverage, for the refreshment of preachers was common. The turning point came in the early 1830s as a result of the growth of the total abstinence movement which came into England from the United States via Ireland. The temperance issue was raised at the Primitive Methodist Conference of 1831, and John Stamp, a Primitive Methodist travelling preacher, took up the cause with rather wild enthusiasm, naming his homestead on Deansgate, Manchester, as Teetotal Cottage. The patient solid work of persuading Primitive Methodism of the virtues not only of temperance but also of total abstinence was done largely by Hugh Bourne. William Clowes, however, never felt any obligation to abstain.

In an often quoted remark, Hugh Bourne is said to have asserted that it was not a case of his joining the temperance movement but of the movement having joined forces with him. This was on the basis that Bourne was already a teetotaller before the Seven Men of Preston (some Primitive Methodists among them) had made their famous pledge in September 1832 to 'abstain from all liquors of an intoxicating quality . . . except as medicines'. That same year the minutes of the Primitive Methodist Conference declared its approval of temperance societies and recommended them to the general membership. Bourne's commitment to the cause, once made, was steady and consistent, and is evidenced in many different ways, ranging from his recipe for non-alcoholic raisin wine for use in Holy Communion to his approval of the enthusiasm shown by Squire Shafto in 1838 in imposing his temperance convictions not only on his entire household but also on the Shafto estates at Bavington (about a dozen miles north of Hexham) where the public house was closed down and replaced by a coffee house.[13]

Hugh Bourne adopted the teetotal stance and promoted it whenever he could on his journeyings throughout the Connexion, joining forces on occasion with local branches of the Rechabites and other total abstinence societies[14] [53]. Primitive Methodist employers who, like Squire Shafto, approved of temperance, were in a position to exercise some degree of control over their workers with regard to the consumption of alcohol, and through various persuasions or pressures to urge them to adopt temperance or even teetotalism. William Hartley, the Primitive Methodist jam maker, was a life-long teetotaller and a strongly paternalist

53. In 1854 the conference received a deputation from the U.K. Alliance and passed a resolution in favour of the object it aims to accomplish. This was probably the first endorsement of the kind given by a powerful religous body in it highest official assembly. But as early as 1832 – in the Minutes as consolidated and embodied at the Conference held at Bradford – we find the following:

Q. 'What is the opinion of Conference in regard to temperance societies?'
A. 'We highly approve of them, and recommend them to the attention of our people in general.'

These facts will show that Primitive Methodism sympathized with the cause of temperance when that cause was less popular than it is now, and that its influence has been exerted in the direction of social reform.

Source: H. B. Kendall, *History of the Primitive Methodist Connexion*, London: Joseph Toulson, 1889, pp. 119–20.

employer anxious for the moral as well as the social well-being of his workforce. Annually he donated sums of money to his employees, as part of his commitment to profit sharing. The allocation of this money was to some extent dependent on a judgement with regard to the moral seriousness of each employee, however, including his or her use of alcohol. Another of his attempts to encourage temperance among his workforce was the provision at Aintree of a café and institute, as a counter-attraction to the public house. Hartley's commitment to the temperance movement was deep, and demanding on his own resources. In one year (1908) he donated £1,000 to the United Kingdom Alliance, and over a period of three years contributed £310 per annum towards the cost of temperance teaching in Liverpool schools. Copies of a book on *Alcohol and the Human Body* by Sir Victor Horsley and Dr Mary Sturge were sent at his expense to every active minister in all the branches of Methodism.[15]

The campaign which was generated in the 1850s

to employ political action to prohibit the trade in intoxicating liquors did not apparently win support from Primitive Methodism, though it was a much debated issue. Concern over the drink trade was acute, but there was a widespread reluctance among nonconformists to encourage state control over areas of private choice, even on such an urgent issue as the drink problem. Joseph Rowntree and Arthur Sherwell emphasized this conviction in their book *The Temperance Problem and Social Reform* (1899), a copy of which was sent via Primitive Methodism's Book Steward to each minister in the Connexion at the arrangement and expense of Sir William Hartley. In the Preface they wrote:

There can be little doubt that if Temperance reform is to advance upon the ordinary lines of social progress in this country, it must do so by giving the localities a large measure of self-government in relation to the drink traffic . . . there must be a real liberation of local forces.[16]

Organized temperance work among the young took some time to develop, but emerged in the Band of Hope Movement whose work in the United Kingdom began in 1855. The Band of Hope pledge was simple and direct: 'I do hereby agree (the Lord helping me) to abstain from all INTOXICATING LIQUORS as beverages, and from the use of TOBACCO and SNUFF, and to discourage the use of them by others.' By the end of the century there were within Methodism three quarters of a million branches of the Band of Hope, 209,000 of them within Primitive Methodism. The results of all this were considerable. Clive Field's researches suggest that virtually all Primitive Methodist ministers, and 90 per cent of local preachers, were total abstainers by 1900. Of the general membership perhaps two thirds abstained from drink about that time, but World War I and the social upheavals of the post-war years were to put increasing pressure on the strict standards with regard to the consumption of alcohol which had been so painstakingly built up in Victorian England.[17]

At the time at which these words were being written it was moving to read in the *Methodist Recorder*, 13 April 2000, of the death at the age of 84 of Horace Mudge. Born in 1915 to staunch Primitive Methodist parents, Horace's career was in administrative and social work with the Independent Order of Rechabites, and later as a civil servant when the Rechabites were absorbed into the National Health Service. The Independent Order of Rechabites, founded in 1835, was a temperance benefit society, offering to acknowledged abstainers financial provisions for sickness, accident and death. For the origin of its name see the book of Jeremiah, 35.1–10.

Home missions

Primitive Methodism's original impetus had come from an urgent sense of calling to renew the mission to the British Isles which John Wesley had originated. Half a century later what had begun by the Primitive Methodists as a missionary movement was assuming the character and style of an established denomination and forming the institutional framework necessary for and appropriate to this development. And yet, while this process was well underway, there came a renewed call to basic 'Home Mission' as a result of the enlargement of Primitive Methodism's work in large towns and cities (including those particularly identified by John Petty as in need of such work) and a sharpened awareness of the challenges to effective Christian work which these communities posed. A growing and widespread conviction by this time was that home mission work required not only evangelism but also a strong social and educational element, as was to be embodied in the Central Hall movement largely inspired by the Wesleyan minister Hugh Price Hughes (1847–1902), the first superintendent of the West London Mission.

While not being able to rival the scale and extent of Wesleyan work in this manner Primitive Methodism had some creditable achievements, among which the work of Thomas Jackson (1850–1932) rates highly. Jackson was born in Belper, where the Primitive Methodists were first called 'Ranters', and he showed a tenacity and vision worthy of comparison with those early pioneers. As a young married man he was invited to become a Primitive Methodist circuit missionary and very soon found himself as a probationary minister at the Bethnal Green Mission, London. He was to serve in the east end of London for the next 56 years. His greatest work was done in Whitechapel, including the establishment of an Institute for Homeless Lads, which was to inspire a London Alderman to exclaim that the three great sights of Whitechapel were the Royal Mint, the London Hospital and the Working Lads' Institute, and that 'The Institute is coining something more precious than the Mint, and if the Hospital mends bodies the Institute repairs lives'. Through a convalescent home, Homes of Rest at Southend, work among prisoners, advice and support to women, and other agencies Jackson and his wife and staff expressed Christian love and care in the most practical of ways.[18]

Another capable city missioner was James Flanagan (1851–1918), a Mansfield coal miner of Irish Catholic extraction who was converted at the Bath Street chapel in Mansfield, became a local preacher, and proved so effective as an evangelist that he was appointed City Missioner for Nottingham. Within a few years he was ordained into the Primitive Methodist ministry and served in Southwark in what was to become the London South East Mission, based in a fine suite of premises in St George's Hall, built for this purpose in 1900. The hall was dedicated to Hugh Price Hughes (1847–1902), chief inspirer from the 1880s of the Wesleyan 'Forward Movement' and its programme of establishing 'Central Halls' in urban working class communities as an attempt to bridge the gap between the churches and the working class. St George's Hall embodied Flanagan's convictions that while the gospel is 'expressed in practical acts' social work ought to be 'a stepping stone to Christ'.[19] Flanagan was later appointed as Primitive Methodism's 'Connexional Evangelist' and advocate of Home Mission. That such a post should be established was an indication that Primitive Methodism's evangelical work was increasingly embodied in institutional arrangements and professional appointments, rather than being the natural life-force of the Connexion as in the pioneering days. Indeed such a development had been foreseen for some time past, both to promote vigorous evangelism and to exercise some control over its wilder exponents [54].

54. In consideration of the evident necessity for revivalistic effort, of the wide spread demand for revivalists, and of the evils at present arising from their employment, we ask whether the time has not fully come when the subject should be taken up and treated as a matter for legislative action. The rapid growth of our community, and consequent increase of business and pastoral responsibility thrown on the regular ministry, render it simply impossible for them to devote that amount of attention to purely evangelistic labours that is required; whereas, by the creation of a special class of evangelists, within our denominational organization, and subject to legal control and discipline, this deficiency would not only be met, but the demand for revivalists would be supplied by a class of persons whose interest would be identified with the stability of the Church, and an obstacle thus be taken out of the way of the prosperity and usefulness of the denomination.

Source: MARAHG, 'Special Religious Revivalism', *Christian Ambassador*, 1875–6, pp. 52–9 (59).

For discussion

1. Can Methodism today have an effective influence on social life, values and relationships?

2. How do we resolve the tensions which arise over the use of alcohol?

3. Is it a surprise that nineteenth-century Methodists helped to generate trade unionism?

4. Discuss some examples of Methodists who have served their local communities as employers, patrons and benefactors. Draw on your own locality as far as possible.

5. Discuss the tensions experienced (a) by Methodist employers and (b) by Methodist workers, especially those who committed themselves responsibly to Trade Unionism.

6. Discuss the significance of the Primitive Methodists' dislike of state interference in the trade in alcoholic drinks.

7

Primitive Methodist Hymnody

The preface of the *Methodist Hymn Book* of 1933, published to serve the newly united Methodist Church, is best remembered for its opening declaration 'Methodism was born in song'. Among Methodists the phrase has become a motto, and virtually a platitude, but Methodist life and worship, and the high quality of its hymnody, cannot be taken for granted any more than the rise of Methodism can. Nevertheless it is no surprise that a fervently evangelical movement, strongly committed to the values of Christian fellowship and the open sharing of deep experience, should break into song, and discover in hymnody a marvellous vehicle for the expression of the love of God and neighbour. That Charles Wesley was on hand to provide Methodism with an inexhaustible stream of fine hymns is no less than a sheer act of Providence.

The early hymn books

From the thousands that Charles wrote John Wesley made various collections, in particular the edition of 525 carefully selected hymns 'For the use of the people called Methodists', published with its famous preface in 1780. It was this collection with which the founders of Primitive Methodism would be very familiar, and naturally they would draw upon its resources in the earlier stages of their movement. In 1809 (the year following his eviction from Methodism by the Burslem Quarterly Meeting) Hugh Bourne published an adaptation of Lorenzo Dow's book under the title *A General Collection of Hymns*

and Spiritual Songs for Camp Meetings, Revivals, etc. of which a number of increasingly enlarged editions were published up to the early 1820s. By that date the need had become apparent for a fuller book to serve the growing number of Primitive Methodist congregations throughout the Connexion, many of them building chapels and establishing a regular programme of congregational life and worship. The Annual Meeting of 1821 called for a new collection (though under the old title) and within a year the book had been prepared by Hugh Bourne and printed at Bemersley by his brother James. It became known as *The Small Hymn Book* to distinguish it from a larger collection published only three years later. There is no clear plan to the small book's contents. It is evangelical in spirit, suited particularly to the requirements and character of the Primitive Methodist Connexion at that time, but lacking in other respects. There is for instance one lone Christmas hymn. Apart from a number of hymns by Watts, Wesley and Newton, the collection seems to be the fruit of Primitive Methodist writers, Hugh Bourne in particular. Some examples may be given to illustrate the character of this book [55].

At the end of the book is a short selection of verses for singing during prayer meetings, a practice insisted on by Hugh Bourne: 'Let the members of the Society pray in quick succession for about 2, 3, or 4 minutes each; with singing a verse or two, occasionally, to vary the exercises'.[1] Primitive Methodist prayer meetings were by no means quiet and contemplative gatherings at this early period. The hope and intention was that the members would get 'into

55. (1)   We, little flock, by all contemn'd,
          O'erlooked, unknown, despis'd, condemn'd.
          With names traduc'd, and lives abhorr'd,
          We suffer with our murder'd Lord;
          Yet, when the flames ascend the higher,
          We'll shout, triumphant in the fire.

                           (No. 3, last verse)

(2)   Thou chusest not the rich and great
      To spread the truth around;
      By foolish men, of low estate,
      Thou dost the wise confound.

      These are exposed to rain and wind,
      While o'er the wastes they roam;
      They leave their dearest friends behind;
      Their kindreds and their home.

      O crown their labours with success,
      Thou God of love divine!
      O condescend their work to bless,
      And be the glory thine.

               (No. 99, three verses out of four)

(3)   How prone are professors* to rest on their
        lees,
      To study their profit, their pleasure and
        ease;
      Tho' God says arise and escape for your
        life,
      And look not behind you – Remember Lot's
        wife
      But if you're determin'd the call to refuse,
      And venture the way of destruction to chuse,
      For hell you will part with the blessing of
        life,
      And then, if not now, you'll remember Lot's
        wife.

        (No. 115, first and last verses out of six)

Source: Small Hymn Book, 1821.

* Professors here refers to those who profess Christianity outwardly
but not from the heart.

faith', and pour out their praise and prayer without restraint, stirring up a revivalistic spirit which could result in conversions within the meeting itself.

A copy of the Primitive Methodist *Small Hymn Book* in the writer's possession has an autograph inside the front cover which reads 'Mary Bell's Hym Book [*sic*], Coanwood July 26th 1823'. Coanwood, a former centre of Quakerism, is a hamlet in the valley of the South Tyne, in south-west Northumberland, and Mary must have been one of the early recruits to the Primitive Methodist cause soon after it reached the Weardale and Tynedale areas late in the year 1822. It is not hard to imagine how the possession of this little hymn book would help to confirm her in her membership of the new movement, and provide a personal resource for her own devotions and discipleship at a time when to throw in one's lot with the Ranters demanded no little courage and commitment. When Kendal was missioned by the Primitive Methodists about this same time, the *Small Hymn Book* made such a strong impression upon an elderly woman that she bought a copy, walked to Carlisle to show it to her friends, and became thereby the instrument in the introduction of Primitive Methodism to that city.[2]

Nevertheless the shortcomings of the *Small Hymn Book* must soon have become obvious to Hugh Bourne, and within four years of its publication *The Large Hymn Book* appeared, containing 536 hymns, in a convenient pocket-sized format, and in some editions bound together with the *Small Book*, which was supplemented, not replaced, by its successor. The book's emphasis remains experiential, rather than ecclesiastical or doctrinal, with 132 hymns devoted to 'prayer and the fight of faith', 67 to 'confidence and joy in God', 43 to 'mourners' (referring here to those who mourned their sins and longed for redemption) and 20 to backsliders. Only 36 are designated specifically for what might be called 'church' use: 4 for the love feast, 6 for baptism, 3 for the Lord's Supper, 5 for Christmas, 3 for Easter and 15 for church openings, anniversaries, etc. Many of the hymns are versified stories from Scripture, usually related to characters from the Old Testament.

Abraham, Moses, Jacob, Goliath, Noah, David and Saul are among those treated in this homely fashion.

The Camp Meeting theme is still pervasive in this book, and crops up in unexpected places, as for instance in a hymn to the Trinity [56]:

> 56. (1) Almighty God in persons three,
>   Camp Meetings have been blessed by Thee
>   (No. 503)
>
>   (2) (And more surprisingly in a vision of heaven:)
>   Our troubles and trials will then be all o'er,
>   The Head of Camp Meetings we there shall
>   adore (No. 501)
>
> *Source: The Large Hymn Book*, 1826.

These hymns are 2 of the 146 which were written by Hugh Bourne and William Sanders for the *Large Hymn Book*. Sanders was born in 1799 and began his working career as a boy on the Bournes's farm at Bemersley. His talents blossomed, and in 1820 he entered the Primitive Methodist ministry, serving in a number of English circuits before sailing to America. He is perhaps best remembered by his hymn 'Hark! the gospel news is sounding', number 16 in the *Large Hymn Book*, where the authorship is credited to Sanders and Bourne jointly[3] [57]. It seems likely, however, that in this case Sanders was the sole author, and is shown as such in the *Methodist Hymn Book* (1933), in which the hymn (no. 315) was included as one which in a special way characterized the Primitive Methodist tradition [58]. It was enormously popular among the Primitive Methodists, especially for marches and camp meetings. In a copy of the *Large Hymn Book* in the writer's possession the pages on which this hymn falls are much more darkened by handling than any others in the entire volume.[4] The *Large Hymn Book* is greatly enhanced by the inclusion of many hymns by some of the best writers. With others by Isaac Watts, William Cowper, Philip Doddridge, John Byrom, Joseph Addison and John Newton, 225 are from the pen of Charles Wesley. Despite these the *Large Hymn Book*

> 57. Hark! The gospel news is sounding,
>   Christ hath suffer'd on the tree;
>   Streams of mercy are abounding,
>   Grace, for all, is rich and free,
>   Now, poor sinner, look to Him who died for thee.
>
>   Oh! escape to yonder mountain,
>   Now begin to watch and pray;
>   Christ invites you to the fountain,
>   Come, and wash your sins away,
>   Do not tarry, Come to Jesus while you may.
>
>   Grace is flowing, like a river,
>   Millions there have been supplied;
>   Still it flows as fresh as ever,
>   From the Saviour's wounded side;
>   None need perish, all may live, for Christ hath
>   died.
>
>   Christ alone shall be our portion;
>   Soon we hope to meet above,
>   Then we'll bathe in the full ocean,
>   Of the great Redeemer's love;
>   All his fulness, we shall then for ever prove.
>
>   Hugh Bourne & William Sanders
>
> *Source: Large Hymn Book*, No. 16.

retains much of the character of the earlier collection, and these two books are essential sources for an understanding of the heart and mind of Primitive Methodism at a stage when it had few, if any, ecclesiastical pretensions.

Before leaving Hugh Bourne's *Large Hymn Book*, its Preface demands our notice. It begins with his vision of the scriptural basis for the 'Service of Song', ranging from the morning stars singing together and the sons of God shouting for joy (Job) to the triumphant chorus of the book of Revelation. From this elevated height Bourne soon comes down to the practicalities of worship.

None should be suffered to take any part in leading the singing service but such as can 'sing with

58. Sanders' hymns are as good an introduction as any to the underlying spirituality of the *Large Book*. Once again however a number of different approaches to this aspect of the Hymnal lie open to us . . . An impressionistic overview is possible, such as is given by John Kent in his book *Holding the Fort* where the vigour of this spirituality is contrasted sharply with the maudlin sentimentality of much later revival hymnody. Kent also remarks on the themes of conflict and violence and the buzz word 'glory', which, emptied of its precise meaning and repeated over and over again, becomes a kind of mantra, an open door to an out-of-body experience, an expression of 'collective effervesence' (Durkheim). The Camp Meeting may indeed have witnessed what modern Pentecostals would be quick to recognise as singing in the spirit which is perhaps why George Borrow always remembered this 'strange sound' which 'tingled in his ears', especially when later in his life he tasted the solemn pomp of the Orthodox Liturgy or the Roman High Mass.

Source: Ian Sellers, *The Hymnody of Primitive Methodism*, 1993.

grace in their hearts unto the Lord' . . . Their zeal is to bring the whole congregation forward in the singing service, to lead them into faith, and enable them, as much as is possible, to sing with the spirit, and with the understanding also, and with grace in their hearts unto the Lord.

Sermons should last about 20 to 30 minutes, and the whole service not exceed an hour and a quarter. In prayer meetings those present should kneel to pray, sit for the preaching, and 'get into faith as much as possible in order that the Holy Ghost may descend'. Similar exhortations are set out for class meetings and the love feast, in which the sharing of bread and water within a context of singing, prayer and shared personal experience is described. Bourne then sets out the ordering of Camp Meetings in detail, drawing on his long and deep practical experience. Finally, he turns to the use of musical instruments in worship, concluding that they should be admitted only with great caution, and that 'none but

decidedly pious persons' should on any account play on them. The Preface is an epitome of the religious nature of Hugh Bourne and of the earnest piety of early Primitive Methodism.

The role in Primitive Methodist hymnody of Richard Jukes (1804–67) must be acknowledged. He served as a Primitive Methodist itinerant for 30 years in Midland circuits and applied his native love of poetry and music in his ministry, publishing many hymns and songs [59]. They sold in large numbers but were sparsely used in the official Connexional hymn books. *The Methodist Hymn Book* 1933 included one, 'My heart is fixed, eternal God'. Jukes's influence was largely spread in informal ways.

59. What Castillo did morally for the dales of Yorkshire, what Waugh did socially for the mill hands of Lancashire, what Wesley did spiritually for the Methodist people . . . and what Mr Sankey's hymns have done for the whole of Christendom of late years, the hymns of Richard Jukes did for our church, and others, half a century ago.

Many an earnest Evangelist has gone to his work singing:–

> I'm a recruiting officer,
> Commissioned from on high;
> I'm one of the great army
> Which does in Zion lie.
> I'm come enlisting soldiers,
> To fight the daring foe:
> Then come, enlist, and with me sing
> I'm bound for to go.

Source: P. M. M., 1903, p. 70.

Tune books and Flesher's hymn book

There was for many years a reluctance to publish a Connexional tune book, largely because of fears that it might offend traditional usage and arouse controversy. Consequently, choirmasters and congregations had to seek out suitable melodies from the common stock of hymnody extant at that time, or produce new tunes of their own. Localized manuscript collections were compiled, including some tunes generally known and others original and often named after places within the area concerned. The field was wide open to individual initiative. At Newcastle upon Tyne in the middle decades of the nineteenth century, John Kidd (born at Garrigill, Cumbria, in 1805) held sway as choirmaster at the central chapels on Silver Street and later Nelson Street, leading the singers and orchestra with his violin, and composing many original hymn tunes, including one for Philip Doddridge's hymn 'O happy day that fixed my choice', which could well be the lively anonymous tune allocated to this hymn in the *Methodist Hymn Book* 1933, number 744.

The evident need for a Connexional tune book finally provoked the publication in 1862 of such a book compiled by a group of Primitive Methodist laymen of Leeds, most notably G. W. Armitage and his brother. Thus challenged, the Primitive Methodist Connexional Book Depot responded within a decade by publishing *The Companion to the Hymn Book*, 'a comprehensive collection of tunes, chants and anthems, selected from the best available collections and enriched with new and original tunes', compiled by Philip Brown. It consisted of 486 hymn tunes grouped according to metre, and was applied to what was, at the time of its publication, the most recent hymn book issued by the Primitive Methodist Connexion, John Flesher's collection published in 1854. Flesher (1801–74) was a Yorkshireman who entered the Primitive Methodist ministry in 1822, serving for 20 years in various outposts of the great Hull Circuit, mainly in the north-eastern counties but including London and Edinburgh, and gathering extra responsibilities along the way.[5] H. B. Kendall comments that 'from 1830 to 1850 John Flesher was one of the busiest and most influential men in our Church-life'. He had tremendous flair, a great appetite for work and responsibility, a passion for detail, and a benign and genial manner coupled with financial independence in his later years which prompted the Connexion to regard him as a gentleman. Renowned as an orator in his younger years, a throat ailment virtually ended his public speaking from 1843 onwards. His wife Jane was a loyal and supportive partner, though their family life was saddened by the early death of one daughter and the lifelong estrangement of another through her breaking the conventions of Primitive Methodism by marrying a minister before the end of his probation.

Flesher showed such versatility that the Connexion believed that no task was beyond him, including the editing of a new hymn book. He had served as Connexional Editor from 1842 to 1852, and in this role had modernized the monthly *Primitive Methodist Magazine* and produced a new edition of the Primitive Methodist *Consolidated Minutes* (1850) with a meticulous and complex index to its contents. Nevertheless the call to edit a hymn book was a challenge which he accepted with strong reservations, and only through the support of his wife Jane whom he enlisted as a partner in his task. The title page of the resulting book explains that it was compiled partly from the *Small* and *Large Hymn Books* of Hugh Bourne and 'from hymns of numerous popular authors (living and deceased) and from those of unknown authors, and enriched with original hymns and selected ones, altered or re-made'. It is those last three words which were to sound the knell of critical doom over Flesher's hymn book, summed up by the Wesleyan hymnologist George J. Stevenson in the entry on 'Methodist Hymnody', in the magisterial *Dictionary of Hymnology*, edited by John Julian (1892): 'This book, issued in 1854 may be safely described as the worst edited and severely mutilated collection of hymns ever published'.[6] It is indeed a shock to look through the book's index and read again and again 'C. Wesley altered', 'Hugh Bourne altered', 'Watts remade', etc. especially when the changes have no justification other than Flesher's whim. And there are, in some editions, other editorial indulgences to incite the critical reader, as in hymn 670, in which eight verses written alternately by Flesher and his wife are given the signature 'John' and 'Jane' respectively after each verse!

Flesher's lapses of judgement and taste aroused strong complaints throughout the Connexion, especially in the north where Colin Campbell M'Kechnie, a learned Scottish minister serving in the Sunderland District, was one of the book's severest critics, and stirred up such animosity towards it as to threaten a major disruption within the Connexion had not John Petty and other moderates wisely intervened.[7] Had the book any saving graces? It came out in a nicely bound edition, about identical in size to the standard words edition of the current *Hymns and Psalms* and rather more elegant. It was well printed, and had full indexes to the hymns and their authors, to the subjects and to the biblical texts relevant to them. Flesher provides a summary phrase at the head of each hymn to indicate its subject matter, and the metre of each hymn is also shown. The book sold well from the start, as a report from the Brigg Primitive Methodist Circuit makes clear: 'The new Hymn Book, compiled by our beloved brother Flesher, is well received in this circuit. Notwithstanding the high price of provisions, 248 copies have already been sold'. It has to be admitted that most worshippers in Primitive Methodist chapels would not be aware of or concerned by the controversy which Flesher's book aroused among its more critical readership. And despite its lapses his book was adequately suited to an evangelical Connexion which was on course to develop into a church, and it served Primitive Methodism usefully enough in the 30-year period during which that transition was to be accomplished. The contributions of Richard Jukes to the book represented the revival hymnody of Primitive Methodism, though certain other hymns which came to be used in this popular mode, such as 'Stop poor, sinner, stop and think', originated from a more classical stable, in this case from the pen of John Newton. Flesher introduced the users of his hymnal to a new generation of early nineteenth-century hymn writers whose work was probably unknown to many. Among them were Reginald Heber, Ray Palmer, James Edmeston, George Washington Doane, Mrs Cecil Frances Alexander and Henry Francis Lyte, an international though largely Anglican group; Palmer was a Congregationalist. Using this book thoughtfully week by week could be an educational experience for Primitive Methodist worshippers.

Later Primitive Methodist hymnody

Before the publication of another major Connexional hymn book two collections of hymns for children appeared, *The Primitive Methodist Sabbath School Hymn Book* of 1863 prepared by the Revd William Antliff, followed by the *Primitive Methodist Sunday School Union Hymn Book* of 1879. Since the previous book catering for children was Hugh Bourne's *Sunday Scholar's Companion*, these new publications were welcome, and indeed overdue. The 1879 book was edited by two Primitive Methodist laymen, George Booth of Chesterfield and William Beckworth of Leeds, the first of whom was to play a major part in the next significant contributions to Primitive Methodist hymnody. These were the *Primitive Methodist Hymnal* of 1887, its *Supplement* of 1912, and the *Primitive Methodist Sunday School Hymnal* of 1901. Booth (1840–1926) was the son of a Primitive Methodist minister who had served in the Midland counties and died when still in active service. His widow ran a small school to assist her son's education, first in pharmacy and then in medicine. Once qualified, George Booth practised entirely in Chesterfield for over half a century, as well as playing a prominent role in the town's religious, civic and educational life.

He was one of the members of the Connexional Committee appointed by the Conference of 1882 to be responsible for the production of a new hymn book, and appears to have emerged as its leading spirit to such an extent as to justify his title as editor. He was assisted by W. T. Brookes (a London businessman) in the preparation of the words edition and by Henry Coward in the revision of the musical harmonization. The contents are ordered clearly and sensibly and there are indexes to hymns, verses, authors and relevant texts where appropriate. The book is large, with 1,052 hymns, yet a *Supplement* of 300 hymns was added in 1912, for which Booth had the assistance of William Heslop of Darlington, who had also assisted in the selection of tunes for the *Hymnal*. Stevenson's comment in Julian on the 1887 hymn book is generous and appreciative [60]:

> 60. It is purely and intensely Methodistic whilst in the number of its authors, in the comprehensiveness of its subjects, in the richness of its poetry, in the care and accuracy displayed in the text, and in the designations of authorship, it has no equal in Methodist hymnody ... The committee have guarded as much as possible against altering the text of the hymns and as a rule have scrupulously adhered to the author's own version, where that could be ascertained. [The ghost of Flesher had been well and truly laid!]
>
> *Source*: John Julian (ed.), *A Dictionary of Hymnology*, London: John Murray, 1892, p. 730.

Joint editions of *Hymnal and Supplement* were published in a remarkably wide range of styles and sizes by the Primitive Methodist publishing house. The smallest and in some ways the most attractive of the publications were the pocket-sized editions bound in soft leather and measuring little more than 5 inches by 2 inches, destined obviously for the pocket or handbag. These weighed about 4 ounces, compared with the 3 lbs weight of the largest (word-only) editions! One format had the hymns printed in two columns on each page, and seems to have served as the model for the standard congregational edition of the post-union *Methodist Hymn Book* of 1933.

The classical hymn writers are fully represented in the *Hymnal* with nearly 300 hymns by the Wesleys, 62 by Watts, 46 by Montgomery, 23 by Doddridge, 19 by Newton, 15 by Heber and 11 by Toplady. Early Primitive Methodist hymnody is represented by 17 hymns by Hugh Bourne and William Sanders. There is a scattering of foreign and Latin hymns in translation, including ancient hymns of the Church. The riches of nineteenth-century hymnody are fully exploited, and represented by writers such as Henry Williams Baker, Horatius Bonar, Josiah Conder, John Ellerton, Frances Ridley Havergal, Reginald Heber, John Keble, Henry Francis Lyte, H. S. B. Monsell, John Mason Neale (in translations), George Rawson and Christopher Wordsworth. Longfellow and Tennyson each have one hymn in the collection. There are no dominant contributors to the *Supplement* but the new names are significant: Edward H. Bickersteth, Elizabeth Clephane, Fanny Crosby, F. W. Faber, William Gaskell, Samuel Greg, F. L. Hosmer, William Walsham How, Jean Ingelow, Christina Rossetti, Harriet Beecher Stowe, John Greenleaf Whittier and Christopher Wordsworth. The inclusion of hymns by these writers is a clear indication of the ecumenical, liberal, scholarly, patriotic, socially conscious and even mystical tendencies of Primitive Methodism in the Edwardian era, at least at its more official and institutional levels, but not confined to them. In the light of all this it is something of a shock to find in the preface of *The Methodist Hymn Book* of 1933 the claim that it is 'the first such book since Wesley's final collection of 150 years ago'.

The *Hymnal* with its *Supplement* was a new book for a new century, and served splendidly to refresh Primitive Methodism with a wave of hymns (by no means all modern) which soon became a staple element in its public worship and private devotion, and no doubt influenced the hymnody of other churches. The latest Wesleyan hymn book at that time, *The Methodist Hymn Book* of 1904, contained nearly one thousand hymns but nevertheless omitted a good many of those which the Primitive Methodist *Supplement* was to include. Among these were 'Blest are the pure in heart' (Keble), 'Courage, brother, do not stumble' (Norman McLeod), 'Of the Father's love begotten' (Aurelius Prudentius, trans. J. M. Neale), 'My song is love unknown' (Samuel Crossman), 'City of God' (Samuel Johnson), 'Come let us sing of a wonderful love' (R. Walmsley), 'O love that wilt not let me go' (George Matheson) and 'O Jesus Christ grow thou in me' (J. C. Lavater, trans. H. B. Smith), all of which, among many others from this book, were to find inclusion in the post-union *Methodist Hymn Book* of 1933.[8]

This chapter has dealt primarily with hymn books

intended for regular congregational worship but in addition to these Primitive Methodism produced a variety of books intended for less formal occasions, such as mission services and revivalist gatherings, especially among the young. One such book was *Joyful Songs*, published in the early 1920s, the product of a committee including prominent ministers and laymen, among them Professor A. S. Peake, who had served also on the *Supplement* Committee. It includes some hymns familiar from the standard collection but is particularly interesting for its revivalist emphasis, typified by such hymns as 'The old, old, story is new', 'The beautiful words of Jesus', 'When you long for Christ to bless, count on Him!' and 'Throw out the Life-Line across the dark wave' whose third verse can typify the whole of this hymn and many of the others:

> Throw out the Life-Line to danger-fraught men,
> Sinking in anguish where you've never been:
> Winds of temptation and billows of woe
> Will soon hurl them out where the dark waters
>   flow.

The spirit of such hymns is in direct succession from that of the earliest song books of Hugh Bourne and William Sanders, and was obviously employed to try to keep alive the conversionist emphasis of early Primitive Methodism, though in a society and setting which were much changed. With a similar aim the *Hymnal* Committee urged that 'much advantage would be gained by an approximate return to the lively vigorous singing which characterized the early period of the history of our Connexion' (*Hymnal*, preface to edition with tunes).

A hymn which appeared on the eve of the outbreak of World War I was Robert Wilfrid Callin's 'O Lord of every lovely thing' [61], a celebration of faith and hope and the beauties of the natural world intended for a Sunday School Anniversary. It might be dismissed as an example of Edwardian optimism, but its author was soon to find himself plunged into the anguish of the Great War. He served as a chaplain from 1916 to 1919 with the Northumberland Fusiliers and experienced the great German offensive in the Spring of 1918, and wrote an account of that time entitled *When the Lantern of Hope Burned Low*.

For discussion

1. Discuss the place of hymnody in the worship, community life and devotion of Methodism.

2. Are we sufficiently imaginative and enthusiastic in our use of hymns in worship?

3. While enjoying our hymn-singing, are we critical enough with regard to our hymn books?

4. Try to track down an early Primitive Methodist hymn book and study its character.

5. Do you think that the broader scope of hymnody in later Primitive Methodist hymn books may have diluted the early evangelical fervour of the movement?

---

61. O Lord of every lovely thing,
     The maker of them all,
     Who from the winter's gloomy wing
     Dost shed the splendours of the spring,
     On Thy great name we call.

     Count us amongst the radiant choir
     That sounds Thy name abroad,
     Set in our hands the heavenly lyre,
     With songs of love our hearts inspire,
     The mighty love of God.

     Until with those who toil and dreamed
     To build Thy kingdom here,
     With those the world hath ne'er esteemed,
     With all the hosts of Thy redeemed,
     We in Thy home appear.

Source: *Methodist Hymn Book*, 1933, No. 587, vv. 1, 4, 5.

8

The Hartley Era (1890–1920)

For three-quarters of a century the chief characteristics of Primitive Methodism, and the main channels of its influence upon religious and social life, were its fervent commitment to traditional styles of evangelism and its mission to, and involvement with, the working classes. Chapter 5 has already revealed the tensions within the Primitive Methodist Connexion as some of its members strove to be true to its traditional character in a society that was rapidly evolving in ways that were distancing young and questioning men and women from the constraints of conservative theology and old-fashioned styles of religious life and thought. One set of questions confronting the Connexion therefore concerned scripture and theology. There were other questions, related to the Connexion's commitment to overseas mission, the improvement of theological training, the modernization and centralization of its administrative system and (at the centre of all these) the readiness of the membership to give more willingly to Connexional causes.

Primitive Methodism had always had a weak Connexional sense; loyalty and financial generosity flowed most strongly in local channels. Moreover, the great chapel-building programme of the latter half of the nineteenth century had left many congregations with serious debts. On top of these they were faced with a rise in ministerial salaries from about £12 a quarter in 1850 to something like £32 a quarter in the later 1870s, plus claims to support overseas missions and the theological institutes in Sunderland and Manchester. The depression of the later 1870s and 1880s accentuated these difficulties. Circuits found it hard to pay their ministers, ministerial pension funds were under serious pressure and theological training had to be cut back by the closure of the Sunderland Institute, leaving the Manchester College to limp along with inadequate funds and staffing. The Connexion's Missionary Society, responsible for the support of missions at home and overseas, was virtually crippled by a debt of some £5,000.

Hartley the man

On to this darkened stage walked the man who, after the Connexion's founding fathers, must be regarded as Primitive Methodism's most illustrious and significant lay leader. Sir William Hartley (he was knighted by King Edward VII in 1908 for his commercial and philanthropic work) was born in 1846 to loyal Primitive Methodist parents at Colne, a small manufacturing town in the Pennine hills of north Lancashire.[1] Shopkeeping and school teaching ran in the family, but William inherited or somehow acquired entrepreneurial instincts of an unusually high order, directed by a Puritan conscience and a keen sense of public usefulness. Over a period of some 20 years after setting up his own grocery business in Colne he evolved his own personal strategies with regard both to business and to public service. Jam-making was begun simply because a supplier defaulted on an order, but he discovered a special talent in having to make it himself. His business grew rapidly and by 1886 was established in large new works at Aintree, where a model village was built for his employees. His wealth had been steadily increasing over the previous years and was to escalate yet higher and higher, far beyond what he could have imagined to be possible. In talking about wealth Hartley often spoke of the need to crush one's selfishness, a phrase which reveals both an awareness of the lure of riches and a stern sense of the higher call to dispose of them usefully and generously. He does seem to have been guided by a brighter star than most other prosperous Methodists and was led to consider ways of disposing usefully of his wealth which went far beyond what might have been expected or imagined.

Of crucial importance in this process was a vow taken by William Hartley on New Year's Day 1877, with his wife's full support, to give each year one-tenth of his gross income towards religious and charitable causes. This 'systematic and proportionate giving' was painstakingly recorded in a series of pocket books which reveal a widening range of benefactions to individuals, churches and needy causes of many kinds.[2] The discipline of charitable giving, initially of a modest scope, without doubt laid the foundations for his later enormous benefactions, of which the Primitive Methodist Connexion was to be the major recipient. By that time, William Hartley's giving was to exceed by far the tenth quoted in his original vow, increasing to something like one-third of his gross income.

Despite Hartley's essentially simple religious nature he had a very sharp business sense and was acutely anxious for good administration within the Primitive Methodist Connexion, and well aware of the progressive elements within it which were pressing for the greater effectiveness and modernization of its working practices. This implied a desire to see a general improvement of its standing as a major element in the religious life of the nation, which became one of Hartley's great concerns. From his teenage years he was increasingly aware of the nature of the Primitive Methodist Connexion, not least through contacts with his Uncle Robert who served as a travelling preacher for almost 40 years. He became the confidant of some of the Connexion's most

progressive leaders, including ministers such as Hugh Gilmore, James Travis and Thomas Mitchell, and the lay biblical scholar Arthur Samuel Peake whom Hartley by a miracle was able to persuade to leave Oxford in 1892 in order to help to train Methodist ministers at the Manchester College.

As he grew older, Sir William's white hair and beard gave him a kindly and benevolent air, somewhat reminiscent of Father Christmas. Indeed, as his benefactions to Primitive Methodism extended in size and scope, he virtually became a Connexional Santa Claus, dazzling Primitive Methodists, who were unused to such philanthropy, by his generosity. But was his massive influence over the Connexion wise and good? Before attempting to answer that question his major services to Primitive Methodism need to be explained, if only briefly. It has to be said that these services were not the result of his own ideas and initiatives alone, but were the product of considerable consultation with other leading members of the Connexion, and in particular a group of very capable ministers with a progressive outlook, notably John Atkinson, Hugh Gilmore, James Travis, Joseph Ritson and Thomas Mitchell. Most of them served

---

62. Bourne Chapel, (Leeds 1st Circuit) with its brave little society, at the dawn of the new century was found struggling with its difficulties of a shifting and unresponsive population and a crushing weight of debt . . . Here is a typical case of chapel and school costing thirty years ago just of £3,000, but left with a debt of £2,500. The flood-time of good trade and high wages among miners had subsided before the trustees could raise any more of the initial cost. From 1877 to 1907 all that could be done by way of reducing the debt was to bring it down to £1,400, at which it stood when the present minister, the Revd F.E. Thistlethwaite, entered the Circuit. But during these thirty years the trustees had paid not less than £2,500 for interest, which had to be raised from year to year in addition to all the cost of maintaining public worship.

Source: W. Beckworth, *A Book of Remembrance: Records of Leeds Primitive Methodism*, 1910, p. 290.

63. This edifice was erected in the year 1839, at the cost of £500, towards which £154 was raised by collections, subscriptions, etc. leaving a debt of £346. For some time it prospered well, but distress in trade, and especially the stopping of the Low Mill, caused many of our members and friends to leave the village in search of employment; this brought the chapel into difficulties, and for several years the trustees struggled hard with it, but despite of all they could do there was £84 of bad interest run up, which, added to the debt already on, left the building £430 in debt. In the year 1851, a vigorous effort was made by the trustees and friends to reduce the above debt, when they succeeded in paying off £110, thus leaving £320 still on. Nevertheless it still could not pay its way, so that we are induced to make another attempt to pay £130 off, thus reducing it to £200. Some of the trustees have nobly come forward to help us, and we have already received £100 towards that sum. The above chapel contains 150 lettable sittings, besides 73 sittings, in all 220. The Sunday School connected with it numbers 83 scholars, and is very promising.

Source: W. J. Robson (ed.), *Silsden Primitive Methodism: Historical Records and Reminiscences*, 1910, p. 494. The chapel referred to is that built at Addingham, near Ilkley in West Yorkshire.

virtually their entire ministries in northern circuits, and obviously were the kind of men Hartley could work with and be guided by. Joseph Ritson in fact was minister for seven years in the 1890s at Aintree, the centre of Hartley's jam-making undertakings. These men were well able to provide Hartley with inside information on the state of the Connexion and its finances [62]. The overall debt on Connexional chapels at the time was in the region of one hundred million pounds in modern values, of which three million pounds were the debt on the chapels of Hull alone. The methods of raising and paying the sums involved were often rough and ready [63]. Joseph Ritson may well have shared with William Hartley the story of his own experience when as a young minister at Blyth he was deputed to carry one thousand gold sovereigns in a weighty bag from Blyth to Berwick where the mortgagee of Blyth chapel met him at the railway station to receive the cash, to the great relief of both parties!

The Chapel Aid Association

It was to overcome such risky and unbusiness-like procedures, and more particularly to provide for Primitive Methodism with both a reliable savings bank and a trustworthy source of loans for chapel building, that the Primitive Methodist Chapel Aid Association was launched. Hartley had devised such a scheme in the 1870s but it was not until 1890 that it became a reality, with Hartley as Chairman and a board made up of ministerial and lay directors. Hartley's plan was that the Association should receive deposits, of any size, at three and a half per cent interest (the Post Office Savings Bank was then paying two and a half per cent) and to make loans to trustees for chapel and school building at three and three-quarters per cent. Despite the tiny profit margin the Association proved to be an instant success and a boon to Primitive Methodist Societies burdened by the cost of chapel erection. Confidence in the Association was of course crucial and it depended largely on the name and reputation of William Hartley who by 1894 had deposited £15,000 of his own money into Chapel Aid. Further than this he made a provision in his will to authorize his executors to deposit in Chapel Aid sufficient money from his own estate to meet any heavy withdrawals that might occur after his death. Hartley died in 1922 but by then the alarm had passed, thanks to the Association's mounting reserves and investments.

The Primitive Methodist Insurance Company had been founded in York in 1865 and the Chapel Aid Board, which had a strong north country representation, decided also to make that city the base of its operations, and to share the Insurance Company's offices and secretary. New premises in York were opened on Telford Terrace in 1900, from where the Chapel Aid Association continues to serve

Methodism today according to the plans of operation laid down by Sir William Hartley in 1890. Indeed the Chapel Aid Association, which was unique in Methodism, is the only organization inaugurated from within Primitive Methodism that has retained fully its individual character in the service of the Methodist Church formed as a result of Methodist Union in 1932.

A plaque within the Chapel Aid offices pays tribute to Sir William's 'sagacity and loyalty', qualities which were evident not only in his work on behalf of the Chapel Aid but also in other vital initiatives on behalf of Primitive Methodism. Overseas missions were a major concern of Hartley, partly due to the cause itself, and partly because once again he felt frustrated and provoked by the reluctance of the Connexion to offer the financial support which was needed. The debt of the Missionary Society by 1884 was in the region of £5,000, and in that year Hartley offered £1,000 towards the elimination of it on condition that the remaining £4,000 would be raised by the Connexion. Something in Hartley's character and the nature of his challenge stirred Primitive Methodists throughout the land and, despite gloomy prognostications, £4,542 was raised by his appeal. In 1890 he was appointed Missionary Treasurer and in that capacity managed to treble the money given by the circuits in support of missions. Moreover, with Thomas Mitchell and James Travis he stumped the country on behalf of the Missionary Jubilee Fund of 1892 (in celebration of the fiftieth anniversary of the setting up of the General Missionary Committee) and helped to raise £50,000 for missionary and other connexional funds, to one of which he contributed £7,500. In 1920 on the occasion of the African Missions Jubilee he donated £5,000. It has to be repeated here that these sums need multiplying by something like one hundred in order to gain some approximate assessment of their value today.

Ministerial training and Dr A. S. Peake

Hartley's role in the extension and improvement of ministerial training was surely his most influential contribution to the improvement of the Connexion's life and work. In other areas his help was largely related to financial and administrative matters, but here he was affecting the mental and spiritual development of future ministers whose influence would permeate the Connexion at large for decades to come and indeed continue into the Methodist Church after the Union of 1932.

In April 1892 Hartley circulated to a large number of ministers and laymen a letter stressing 'most strongly the importance of the better education of our young ministers, believing it to lie at the very root of our future Connexional prosperity'. His enthusiasm for this cause had not always burned so brightly, and had been expressed up to this date in quite modest gifts of money to the Manchester College. The turning point is best described in the words of one who was to be fully involved in the consequences of Hartley's change of heart, Arthur Samuel Peake [64].

The consequences of this outwardly fortuitous meeting were great, largely due to the impact upon Hartley of A. S. Peake's own scholarship and ability, and the force of his case in favour of major reform of the Primitive Methodist theological college in Manchester. Within a very short while Hartley

---

64. In May 1891 Mr and Mrs Hartley were taking a driving tour. They stayed for a few days in Oxford and my friend, Mr J. Harryman Taylor, who was training for the Primitive Methodist ministry at Mansfield College, brought them round to my rooms at Merton College . . . They lunched with me on the Monday. It happened that I had at this time been thinking a good deal about the training which was being given at the Manchester College. I was profoundly dissatisfied with the situation. The length of the course, one year, was quite inadequate, the curriculum was antiquated and reactionary. I spoke about the matter to my guests with freedom . . . Mr Hartley was very much interested.

Source: A. S. Peake, *The Life of Sir William Hartley*, 1926, pp. 133–4.

devised a plan, which the Connexion was persuaded by him and others to accept. It resulted in Peake's removal to Manchester as the College's tutor (his salary paid by Hartley for the first five years), the doubling in size by 1897 of the college buildings (paid for by Hartley at a cost of £12,500) and the extension of the college course to two years, with an undertaking to make it three as soon as possible. In 1906, Hartley paid out a further £20,000 to enlarge the college yet again, thus trebling the size of the student community from what it had been before Hartley's reforms, and allowing for a three-year course. Capable of housing 105 students, the college could now send out some 35 men a year into the active ministry, thus meeting normal Connexional requirements, and ensuring that all future Primitive Methodist ministers could receive a college training.

It is worth emphasizing that what William Hartley achieved for the college (which from 1906 and in recognition of his magnificent philanthropy bore his name as Hartley College) was a fulfilment of the best hopes of the early pioneers of Primitive Methodist theological education Colin M'Kechnie, Thomas Southron and James Macpherson. In their day these men were obliged to accept minimal or partial achievements through force of circumstance, but their aspirations were always towards a thorough, extensive and demanding education for all Primitive Methodist ministers to equip them personally, mentally and spiritually for their calling.

Hartley's own concern to achieve this end led him into further acts of generosity by offering to pay the extra expenses involved when students wished to extend their course in order to take B.A. and B.D. degrees, and to finance the appointment of college tutors with specialist qualifications. The most notable of these tutors was Hartley's personal recruit Dr Arthur S. Peake, who served the college under nine different Principals from 1892 to 1929 [65]. Within this period he also lectured to Congregational students at the nearby Lancashire Independent College over a period of 17 years. In 1904, he was appointed to be the first Rylands Professor of Biblical Criticism and Exegesis in the University of Man-

65. Perhaps it was Peake's greatest service not merely to his own communion but to the whole religious life of England that he helped to save us from a fundamentalist controversy such as that which had devastated large sections of the Church in America. He knew the facts which modern study of the Bible had brought to light. He knew them and was frank and fearless in telling them, but he was also a simple and consistent believer in Jesus, and he let that be seen too; therefore men who could not always follow him were ready to trust him and let him go his own way. If the Free Churches of England have been able without disaster to navigate the broken waters of the last thirty years, it is largely to the wisdom and patience of trusty and trusted pilots like Arthur Samuel Peake that they owe it.

Source: John Thomas Wilkinson (ed.), 'Arthur Samuel Peake: Biographical Sketch', *Arthur Samuel Peake, 1865–1929: Essays in Commemoration by Elsie Cann, W. E. Farndale . . . [and others], and Selections from His Writings*, London: Epworth Press, 1958, p. 12.

chester and was the principal advocate of the formation of the University's Faculty of Theology. Peake's influence and achievements dominated not only the religious outlook of his fellow Primitive Methodists but also of thinking people in all the churches, helped by his stature as a scholar and his ecumenical spirit. He was essentially a biblical scholar, with a particular interest in the Old Testament, and cheerfully took on the task of introducing his students and readers to the critical approach to scripture, with results that were wide and deep.

In recognizing all this it is necessary to acknowledge also the wisdom and Christian insight of W. P. Hartley in discerning the potential of Peake's future services to Primitive Methodism and in persuading him to leave the pleasant pastures of Oxford for Manchester where his greatest contributions to biblical scholarship were to come to fruition. Of his massive output (which includes a fine biography of Sir William Hartley (1926)) his famous *Commentary on the Bible* (1919), widely known simply as 'Peake's Commentary', must bear the palm. Over one thousand pages long, with an index of 68 pages, each with three columns of annotations, it is an enormous achievement and quickly became a standard reference book for generations of theological students, ministers, local preachers and teachers. The respect in which it was held was acknowledged over 40 years later when an even larger Biblical Commentary, edited by Matthew Black and H. H. Rowley, and bearing the fruits of two generations of biblical scholarship since Peake, was nevertheless published as *Peake's Commentary on the Bible*, as a tribute to 'the Peake tradition of accurate and reliable popular scholarship, and the aim and purpose of the original Commentary' (Preface to Black

and Rowley, p. ix). Peake's own writing was clear and compelling, and affirmed that faith, while being at the heart of Christian experience, should also be reasonable [66].

Peake was never confined to the ivory tower of scholarship. He was a life-long total abstainer and was willing to take to the platform (either in a humble chapel or the Free Trade Hall in Manchester) to advocate the temperance cause. He was so moved by reading *The Bitter Cry of Outcast London* that he almost decided to became a slum priest. And he urgently pleaded the cause of just treatment to Conscientious Objectors during World War I, among them the Primitive Methodist educationist Victor Murray. It is also refreshing to know that with all his great scholarship and academic achievements he had a passion for 'Penny Dreadfuls' and detective stories!

Hartley's philanthropy

To round off this broad survey of the influence and bounty of Sir William Hartley within the Primitive Methodist Connexion, his generosity in assisting the purchase in 1908 of the Holborn Hall in London to serve as a central headquarters and publishing house deserves notice, as does the gift of the two initial pairs of Primitive Methodist Orphan Homes at Harrogate about that same time. Moreover, due to his pride in Primitive Methodism and his eagerness to raise its public profile, he did much to foster the full celebration of the Primitive Methodist Centenary, towards which he donated £15,000. Owing to some uncertainty as to which date to recognize, the celebrations were spread over three years, 1907–10, during which Sir William served as President of the Primitive Methodist Conference for the year 1909–10, when his vice-president was the Revd John Welford who in most respects acted virtually as President. Hartley was only the third layman known to have served as President of the Primitive Methodist Conference, the others being James Bourne in the very early years

---

66. It is not in virtue of holding this or that theory of the Atonement that we are saved, but by the Atonement itself apart from any explanations that theologians may put upon it. But this is not to say that because the theory of the Atonement is not that which saves us, it is therefore unimportant. We may be quite sure that what cannot be commended to our reason can have no permanent hold upon our faith; and if we give up the attempt to reach any kind of conception as to the spiritual principles which underline it, it is not unlikely that sooner or later we may be driven to surrender the fact itself.

Let us be sure that this great thought of the identification of Christ with us and of ourselves with Christ is the key which, while it will not solve all the problems for us, will nevertheless solve them thus far, that we shall be brought to see that the Atonement is in harmony with the great moral principles which we recognise as governing the universe and with the great spiritual principles for which our own nature calls out. And having learnt that great truth, we are brought to a point where the leap of faith and acceptance of Jesus as our own personal Saviour, to whom we owe everything and who has done all for us, becomes not an irrational leap, but one in harmony with the deepest realities of the universe.

Source: J. C. Mantripp, 'Reprinted Papers of Dr Peake', *The Aldersgate Magazine*, 112, October 1931, pp. 605–6.

and Thomas Bateman who served twice, 1857–8 and 1867–8.

A final example of Hartley's initiative ought to be acknowledged. This was the endowment in 1897 of an annual lecture to be given by a Primitive Methodist scholar. The first lecture to be published was a study of 'The Fatherhood of God', by Dr John Watson, which appeared in 1898. The lecture was given annually thereafter (except in time of war) and at Methodist Union was united with the Wesleyan equivalent to become known as the Fernley-Hartley Lecture.

How are we to assess the influence of Sir William Hartley, 'our prince of benefactors', upon Primitive Methodism? What is very obvious is that he vastly improved the institutions of the Connexion, improved the education and general training of its ministers, put its finances in better order, encouraged missions, improved its chapels and generally elevated its status. It seems fair to say that Primitive Methodism was able to enter the prolonged negotiations leading to Methodist Union in 1932 with greater pride and self-confidence as a result of all that Hartley had been able to achieve on the Connexion's behalf. A. S. Peake once said of the improvements made by Hartley to Primitive Methodist theological training that 'Cinderella came into the limelight'. In a sense this was true of the entire Connexion at that time.

Nevertheless there were doubters, mainly composed of those members of the Connexion who looked back with yearning to the evangelical simplicity of early Primitive Methodism. The coincidence of the Primitive Methodist centenary with the climax of Hartley's massive benefactions helped to sharpen the contrast between the increasingly ecclesiastical character of modern Primitive Methodism and the images of the age of Bourne and Clowes which the centenary literature was energetically publicizing. To put it rather crudely, the critics of modernization could see in Hartley's influence the elevation of ministerial status, the centralization of policy-making at the expense of local freedom and initiative, the undermining of traditional conservative evangelical-

ism in favour of modern liberal and critical attitudes, and the encouragement of fine and expensive chapels to replace the humbler tabernacles of an earlier age. There was some justice in these doubts and reservations, and Hartley was not unaware of them. He himself was troubled by the personal influence which he held within the Connexion and felt that too much reliance was placed on him to resolve its problems. Nevertheless he sincerely desired the improvement of the Connexion according to the best light he had, and he certainly found a ready response among many Primitive Methodists whose interests and inclinations were in tune with his own. He was able to join and encourage a current of opinion which was already moving within the Connexion, promoting its modernization. In the words of A. S. Peake, Sir William Hartley 'struck with unexampled force into the stream of our denominational life, lifting its quality to higher levels, accelerating the pace of its progress, making possible otherwise impracticable enterprises'. But Peake went on to stress that despite

> a magnificent loyalty to Primitive Methodism Hartley was by no means a narrow denominationalist. From the sectarian temper, from petty jealousies and rivalries, he was singularly free. He took the keenest interest in interdenominational organisations, he sought the prosperity of other Churches, he was keen on all movements for healing division, he was for many years a powerful and convinced advocate of Methodist union.[3]

For discussion

1. Early Primitive Methodism had a weak Connexional sense. What might have been the positive and negative results of this?

2. Are Methodists today clear-minded about the role of Bible study and ready to undertake an informed approach to scripture in the light of modern scholarship?

3. Try to imagine how differently Primitive Methodism might have developed in its later stages without the patronage and influence of Sir William Hartley.

4. Is it some surprise to you that Primitive Methodism produced a fine biblical scholar, open to modern scholarship, in the person of Dr A. S. Peake?

9
The Primitive Methodist Centenary

In the closing years of the nineteenth century and the opening years of the twentieth one can sense within Primitive Methodism both a deserved pride at what the Connexion had achieved and a keen anticipation of growth and development yet to come. A phrase of scripture from 1 Samuel 7.13, 'Hitherto hath the Lord helped us', expresses the mood of the Connexion at this time, and was much used in the Centenary literature. Primitive Methodism, while not complacent, was at ease with itself and glad to be acknowledged and appreciated as a major denomination, indeed as a church, which was increasingly the description used in the Connexional literature.

Another text favoured by the Primitive Methodists at this time to express the character of the Connexion's achievements was 'What hath God wrought!' (Acts 21.19). This conviction, and the fruits of it, were to be fully affirmed and illustrated through the printed word as we shall see. Nevertheless the fact is that one of the most striking and popular representations of Primitive Methodism at that period was a painting.

A Primitive Methodist painting

The artist in question was William Holt Yates Titcomb, R.B.A. (1858–1930), son of the first bishop of Rangoon and a close friend of the painter Henry Tidmarsh whose Wesleyan membership and Socialist inclinations may have influenced Titcomb in his choice of subject matter. His painting dates from the early 1890s and shows the interior of the Primitive Methodist chapel on Fore Street, St Ives, where Titcomb lived for part of each year. The occasion depicted appears to be a prayer meeting following a summer evening preaching service. The preacher stands in the high pulpit, and below him is a remnant of the original congregation, including in the foregound some chattering boys and two elderly fishermen dressed in their simple workaday garb, and shown in attitudes of prayer on the plain wooden benches [67]. The picture's simplicity, naturalness and integrity assured its wide appeal, and the Primitive Methodist Church readily acclaimed it as 'a nation's picture'.

It is difficult to assess how quickly and widely the painting became known, whether among the general public or among Primitive Methodists in particular. The process seems to have been slow, but by the early 1930s a coloured print came on the market as part of a series of reproductions under the title *Modern Masterpieces of British Art*, published by The Amalgamated Press, London.[1] About the same time monochrome prints appeared as frontispieces to Aquila Barber's *A Methodist Pageant*, and to *Mow Cop and the Camp Meeting Movement*, by Arthur Wilkes and Joseph Lovatt.[2] By that time the original painting had been acquired by the Art Gallery at Dudley, where it can still be seen. However, to Aquila Barber, the Primitive Methodist's Connexional Editor, it was 'a nation's picture', and this proud claim would certainly have had warm approval throughout the Connexion.

The popularity of Titcomb's painting was, without doubt, due to its nostalgic appeal. It conjured up an

67. *The Prayer Meeting* This was true to type whether in Cornwall or in Northumberland. No evening service in those days was complete without its prayer meeting. After the service itself had finished and the preacher had pronounced the Benediction, another hymn was given out and while it was being sung those who had to leave did so, and the remainder came up to the front. As the evening service was intended for the ingathering of sinners it was assumed that some of these would have been so moved by the exhortation during the service that they would have stayed behind. The hymn therefore, with which the prayer meeting began, had to be on a moving or warning note, specially addressed to them.

'Come ye sinners poor and wretched', or
'Why unbelieving, why wilt thou spurn,
Love that so gently pleads thy return?'

(*Primitive Methodist Hymnal*, nos 264
and 252)

Source: A. Victor Murray, *A Northumbrian Methodist Childhood*, ed. G. E. Milburn, Northumberland County Library, 1992, p. 65.

image of Primitive Methodism which was not untrue, but was hardly typical of the Connexion by that date, except in quiet rural corners. Nevertheless it struck a chord in the hearts of many, and reminded them of the basic simplicities of Primitive Methodist devotion and discipline to which they strove to be true, despite the material and intellectual advances which were strong features of the Connexion at that period. The original drawing of the picture was offered for sale at £15 in 1890, and the painting itself for £250 two years later. This was Titcomb's most expensive work up to that date and it must have helped to influence his acceptance as a member of the Royal Society of British Artists in 1892.

Despite the popularity of this painting it was through literature of various kinds that the Primitive Methodist Church most fully publicized and celebrated its centenary. The character and quality of this published material ranged widely from the homely and nostalgic to the instructive and scholarly. The former category included much fictional writing through which an attempt was made, earnestly if romantically, to conjure up the character of chapel life and of Christian obedience in workaday settings. Thus we find serialized in the *Primitive Methodist Magazine* novels such as Joseph Hocking's *Lest We Forget*, J. Dodd Jackson's *The People of the Haven* and W. M. Patterson's *Colliery Village Life*, to name a few. In similar vein were the productions of the Revd J. G. Bowran (1869–1946) under whose pen-name of Ramsay Guthrie appeared such novels as *The Canny Folks o' Coal-Vale*, *Black Dyke* [68], and *The Doctor's Daughter*. It has to be said that as well as being a popular novelist Bowran was a very able and practical circuit minister.

68. Mary Fraser was eaten up with zeal. She was possessed with one idea. Morning, noon, and night, one desire held her captive. For 'Fraser' to 'get religion' was her all-absorbing prayer. She could see the blank line for his name wherever she turned. It was on the wall and on the ceiling. It was in the cupboard and in the fire. She knew that she could never have peace of heart until his name stood above hers in the class-book. She regarded herself as responsible for his conversion.

Source: Ramsay Guthrie (J. G. Bowran), *Black Dyke*, 1904, p. 140.

Centenary histories

The Centenary also stimulated factual historical productions, some of them of a considerable size and solidity. A good example is the 600-page compilation of the records and reminiscences of *Silsden Primitive Methodism*, edited by the Revd W. J. Robson (1910). This is a remarkably full and detailed account with many photographs. Somewhat slighter is *Northern Primitive Methodism*, by W. M. Patterson, 1909, surveying in a romantic style the 'rise and progress of the circuits in the old Sunderland District'. Patterson had much local knowledge to draw upon and valuable records at his disposal but does not divulge them. One fears that many have been lost. Another local account is James Myers's *Eventide Review* of Primitive Methodism in the Otley Circuit, published in 1930 but looking back well into the nineteenth century.

Towering over the entire corpus of historical writing inspired by the Primitive Methodist centenary is H. B. Kendall's massive two-volume work, *The Origin and History of the Primitive Methodist Church*, published in the first decade of the twentieth century. Holliday Bickerstaffe Kendall (1844–1919) came from a Lincolnshire family which in his father's generation had given six of its sons to the Primitive Methodist ministry. Kendall was happy, indeed eager, to follow in their footsteps, beginning to preach as a boy, and entering the Primitive Methodist ministry at the age of 19. At a cost to his own health he combined the arduous round of a travelling preacher in various north-eastern circuits with a self-imposed programme of hard reading and educational improvement which resulted in the award of a B.A. degree from London University as an external candidate. A breakdown finally released him from circuit work and led to commitments more congenial to his talents and his love of scholarship, in particular his appointment as Primitive Methodism's Connexional Editor, from 1892 to 1901. A desk job in which writing and study were everyday requirements, and with the Connexional archives at his disposal, offered Kendall a heaven-sent opportunity to indulge his scholarly and historical inclinations by writing a history of Primitive Methodism.

He began in 1889 with a pocket-sized book which proved to be the essential model for later and vastly enlarged versions. This early book also reveals Kendall's aims in his historical writing: 'Surely not a catalogue of names and dates though arranged with never so much relation to truth and chronological order, but an honest attempt to convey a life-like impression of the method and surroundings, the toils and struggles of our founders and fathers'.[3] Within a dozen years or so Kendall was ready to begin publishing his huge two-volume *Origin and History of the Primitive Methodist Church*, at first in monthly parts. The final outlay by the Primitive Methodist Connexion in this great endeavour must (in modern terms) have been measured in millions of pounds.

The book is not ideal. There is no table of contents, no list of sources, a paucity of references, an inadequate index and a serious imbalance in the distribution of its material, devoting 900 pages to the first four decades of Primitive Methodism's early development, and only 200 pages to the following 60 years. Moreover Kendall seems to have been unwilling to comment objectively upon the nature of Primitive Methodism and its place within the wider spectrum of English ecclesiastical life; and some of its failings and inner tensions are ignored or glossed over. This said, Kendall's great work is a very remarkable achievement. His knowledge of Primitive Methodism's people and places, his insight into the origins and development of the Connexion, and the local settings in which it took root, demand the highest admiration. The use of voluminous illustrations both of people and of places is another great asset of Kendall's work.

The writing and reading of Primitive Methodist history could not be separated from the evangelical spirit which the Connexion had embodied from its beginnings. So it is not surprising that the last years of the nineteenth century and the early years of the twentieth were marked by the outbreak of local and spontaneous revivals, generally focussed upon particular chapels or circuits where the members were earnestly longing and praying for this very end. Middlesbrough offers an example, with the chapel on Gilkes Street its epicentre. The date was 1897, when the circuit ministers were William Younger and Robert Hind, both north country men. They were not apparently the direct agents of the revival, and in fact were surprised by its development, though appear to have given their support once it began, Younger in particular. Emotional love feasts, charismatic gatherings, strange expressions and experiences were all features of the revival, which was apparently not 'engineered' in any particular way but grew out of the regular work of the circuit.

Celebrations

The instinct to try to recreate the fervent experiences of early Primitive Methodism, as its centenary approached, was strong and became a powerful influence upon the planning of the celebrations. As Primitive Methodism had begun in the open air, the planning of the centennial became focussed around a grand Camp Meeting on Mow Cop in May 1907, to be repeated three years later in 1910. The chief themes of the centennial celebrations were to be gratitude, renewed evangelism, personal dedication, the recovery of the old spirit, and the dissemination of knowledge on Primitive Methodism's history and character [69]. The first meeting attracted 90,000 and was claimed to be the largest open-air gathering in Christian history. Even with four preaching stands it cannot have been easy to hear the preachers but large indoor meetings supplemented the open-air events. The atmosphere and the setting of the gathering, high above the Cheshire plain, obviously generated strong and moving emotions among all those present, and a vivid awareness of the origins and character of original Primitive Methodism. A spate of volumes related to Primitive Methodist history and biography was published to supplement the Mow Cop events. Of these Joseph Ritson's *Romance of Primitive Methodism* alone sold 30,000 copies. The total of all sales was half a million.

William Hartley threw himself into the cele-brations with gusto, and in particular encouraged generous giving to Primitive Methodist Connexional causes by his offer to give £15,000 if the Connexion could raise £100,000. In fact three times this sum was raised, £70,000 from Primitive Methodist central funds and £230,000 from the districts and circuits throughout the Connexion. This sum included £10,000 which was donated, despite their modest stipends, by the ministers of the Connexion. Lay people gave as they could, and there are touching stories of generosity such as that of an elderly woman in the Norwich Circuit who donated the first payment of her old age pension (newly introduced) to the Centenary fund. Of the Districts, Manchester, West Midlands and Newcastle/Sunderland raised the largest sums. The money was allocated to all the various departments of the Primitive Methodist Connexion's work, from Sunday Schools to Overseas Missions.

The basic statistics of the Home Connexion at that date were as follows:

Districts	25
Circuits	741
Societies	5,126
Ministers	1,153
Home Missionaries	43
Members	210,173
Chapels (plus rented rooms)	4,509
Sunday Schools	4,209
Teachers	61,275
Sunday Scholars	477,114

Planning of the Centenary began in 1903 and a committee of something like one hundred ministers and laymen was convened with the Revd John Welford as its Secretary [70]. A sense of gratitude for what Primitive Methodism meant permeated the Connexion and was immediately conceived as having a strongly financial element, with an aim to raise £250,000. Three fifths were to be allocated to local projects and the rest to wider Connexional needs. In the event the money was raised more readily for the former, and it fell to Sir William Hartley to remind

69. One of the distinguishing glories of Primitive Methodism was its open-airness, its naturalness, its simplicity, its love of the highways and hedges, its fondness for the field ... It was because Wesleyan Methodism wished to confine us to Barracks that our expansive souls revolted and we raised the cry 'To your tents, O Israel!', and we went out to hold our Camp Meetings in the open field.

Source: J. D. Thompson, *The Church That Found Herself*, 1911, p. 73.

Primitive Methodists, especially the wealthier ones, that 'We believe in emotion but let us transfer our emotion to our pockets. Middle class Methodists should watch and be careful lest as their circumstances improve they spend money in useless luxuries'.[4]

> 70. We deem it to be fitting that in the years 1907 to 1910 we should arrange a series of Centenary Celebrations, not for the demonstration of our strength, but for the promotion of a deeper spiritual life among our people, the inauguration of a great evangelistic movement and the adoption of such aggressive measures as may utilise most fully the possibilities at our hand.
>
> We recognise that for the ends of service in the Kingdom of Christ we carry more into the twentieth century than our fathers did into the nineteenth; but 'the Lord was with them,' and caused them greatly to triumph. It is incumbent on all our people to fitly commemorate our century of history by a new departure in personal dedication to our Lord, in a firmer hold of the great evangelical verities, and in a more strenuous use of our opportunities in pushing the conquests of grace and truth in the world.
>
> *Source*: A statement by Henry Youll (Primitive Methodist Editor) on behalf of the Committee convened to oversee the Primitive Methodist Centenary celebrations. Quoted in Thompson, *The Church That Found Herself*, p. 8.

It was an inspired move by the organizers of the Centenary to launch it at a Camp Meeting on the very site where Primitive Methodism had begun one hundred years before, on the hill called Mow Cop in Staffordshire. A similar gathering took place three years later to round off the Centenary celebrations [71][72]. The public reaction to these occasions was quite remarkable; even tough-skinned journalists were moved by the splendid site, the eager crowds and the warmth and sincerity of the open-air worship, especially the singing. A journalist of *The Morning Leader* in the issue of 27 May 1907 summed it up enthusiastically:

Primitive Methodists, if they sought all the Kingdom for a meeting place that should symbolise their bluff and rugged faith, would have to come to Mow Cop at last. It is the very hill. But they had not to seek it. It came to them by inspiration. It is Rome, Canterbury, and Mecca to them, and more also.

> 71. From four preaching stands, from Saturday afternoon right on to Monday evening there was poured a ceaseless stream of evangelical eloquence, and the air was vocal with holy and passionate song. Before the 1907 meetings were held many had feared that the occasion would degenerate into a kind of religious picnic, and that a spirit of vain glory or a blind worship of the past might mark the time. But in the event not one of these apprehensions was realised. The religious reverence shown was remarkable. The immense crowds were worshipping crowds. The spiritual note was predominant . . . there was cheerfulness and even mirth, but it was sober and without levity, happy but devout.
>
> *Source*: Thompson, *The Church That Found Herself*, p. 16.

> 72. Evening meetings at Hanley and Tunstall followed the open-air gatherings. Six of the Primitive Methodist members of Parliament addressed an audience of 3,000 people. Sir William Hartley, Dr Samuel Peake, Revd James Travis and other leading Primitive Methodists, addressed the gatherings which were repeated in similar style in 1910. Sir William Hartley played a prominent role in the evening meetings where he made one of his generous financial gestures on behalf of the Primitive Methodist Connection, offering an additional £15,000 if the Connection could raise £100,000. Yet despite all the enthusiasm of the great centenary Camp Meetings the Connection had to face the hard fact that a process of diminishing membership had begun. The Primitive Methodists were not alone in this; most of the Free Churches were also reporting a decline.
>
> *Source*: Thompson, *The Church That Found Herself*, pp. 38–9.

For discussion

1. Try to track down sources on the history of Primitive Methodism, and biographical studies of its various leaders.

2. If possible visit chapels in your locality which were built by the Primitive Methodists. Estimate their character and quality and study any memorials and windows. You might even try to research the history of one of them.

3. Try to see a copy of Titcomb's painting of Primitive Methodists and consider its character and message.

4. Visit, if you can, the heartlands of Primitive Methodism at Mow Cop, and the Museum of Primitive Methodism at nearby Englesea Brook.

5. Try to find literature related to the Primitive Methodist centenary. (Examples of relevant books mentioned in this book can turn up in second-hand shops and chapel book sales!)

6. What do we learn about the character of Primitive Methodism in the late nineteenth and early twentieth centuries from its abundant publishing of fiction?

10

Towards Union

A growing sense of disunity within Methodism had begun to well up in the third quarter of the nineteenth century, gathering strength from then on. This movement of feeling inspired a series of conferences, designated as 'ecumenical', largely devoted to drawing together the various strands within Methodism, in Britain and America. The first took place in 1881 and was mainly Wesleyan in representation. The second was held in the USA, and at the third, held in Wesley's Chapel, London in 1901, there were strong expressions of the relative futility of the progress of Methodist unity up to that date [73]. An impatient outburst came from Dr Thomas Bowman Stephenson (1839–1912), President of the Wesleyan Conference of 1891 and founder of the Wesley

---

73. Speaking for myself only, it appears to me that we have got just about as far in inter-denominational fellowship as we are likely to get. We may continue as we are, and we may even somewhat improve our relationship to each other, but I believe we have reached the point at which any serious further advance spells union and nothing less ... In my judgement if any serious further advance in the direction of Inter-denominational Fellowship is desired, it is only possible by way of union, and we may well ask, shall we have grace and sense and wisdom to do the right thing under these circumstances. Pray God we may!

Source: R. Newman Wycherley, *The Pageantry of Methodist Union*, London: Epworth Press, 1932, p. 200, quoting Dr T. B. Stephenson's declaration at the third Methodist Ecumenical Conference, 1901.

Deaconess Order and the National Children's Home and Orphanage.

The approach of a new century both in calendar years, and in the life-story of Primitive Methodism itself, encouraged a range of new and broader initiatives within the Connexion. Examples of some of these are mentioned briefly here to indicate the developing Connexional character, and others can be found in earlier pages:

1878 The Wesleyan Methodist Conference conceded the admission of lay representatives and thereby 'removed the biggest single constitutional difference between the English Methodist denominations, and involved a definite break with the traditional Wesleyan view of the ministry' (J. Kent, *The Age of Disunity*, London: Epworth Press, 1966, p. 1).

1893 The Bethel Primitive Methodist Chapel in Sheffield was converted into a Central Mission, starting a trend within Primitive Methodism which was already well established in Wesleyan Methodism.

1899 A lady delegate was included for the first time in the Primitive Methodist Conference.

1902 'Church' replaced 'Connexion' on Primitive Methodist class tickets, etc.

1904 The Primitive Methodist Church launched a scheme to organize and improve the training of local preachers.

1907 Three Methodist Connexions, the New Connexion, the Bible Christians and the United Methodist Free Churches came together to form the United Methodist Church. Its name was somewhat misleading and it should not be confused with the church which was to result from the major negotiations of the early 1930s, referred to simply as the Methodist Church.

1908 A Social Service Union within Primitive Methodism was inaugurated.

1910 The closing year of the protracted Primitive Methodist Centenary brought a sense both of achievement and the need for change and new beginnings.

Other developments of this kind have been outlined in previous pages, resulting in particular from the initiatives of Sir William Hartley. What is clear is that they were related to concerns and initiatives common to all the Methodist Connexions. Hence the persistent and growing concern among many Methodists for the necessity of mutual cooperation to tackle the growing challenges.

A significant development in the early years of the twentieth century was the adoption of the name 'Primitive Methodist Church' in preference to 'Primitive Methodist Connexion'. As early as 1902 'Primitive Methodist Church' appeared in the Primitive Methodist Consolidated Minutes and on the class tickets which were the formal evidence of personal membership. There can be no doubt that the vast influence of Sir William Hartley upon the organization, status and confidence of Primitive Methodism was a powerful lever in the adoption of the name Church. Having attained this name, Primitive Methodists were eager to display the character and confidence which it inspired, including a readiness to enter into discussions with the other two Methodist Connexions on the issue of unity.

A preliminary to full Methodist Union was the uniting in 1907 of the Methodist New Connexion, the Bible Christians and the United Methodist Free Churches to form the United Methodist Church of Great Britain. It had a short independent lifespan of 25 years but was a major step towards full Methodist Union. Further pressure to this end came from the Fourth Ecumenical Conference held at Toronto in 1911. The English Wesleyan Church showed a willingness to take up the ecumenical baton and invited the United Methodist and Primitive Methodist Churches to follow suit. A Committee of Wesleyan Methodists, Primitive Methodists and United Methodists was formed and a scheme for unity went out, aiming at a vote on Union in 1931.

The progress of the idea of Methodist unity in Britain began to gather pace from this time on, initially under Wesleyan leadership, but by 1913 the three major British Methodist Connexions had made a commitment to it. The leadership of the movement at that time was largely in Wesleyan hands, with the hope that the Primitive and the United Methodists would throw in their lot with similar enthusiasm. In 1918, the Wesleyans made a proposal that they and the other two major Methodist Connexions should seriously explore the avenues towards Union. Their aims were not limited to organizational arrangements only, but to a sincere spiritual fusing of the divisions within the wide Methodist family.

These developments had taken place under the shadow of the first World War. The major impact of war on the churches was the result of the recruitment of large numbers of men into the forces, and the risks of active service. Of the Primitive Methodists

---

74. My duties were innumerable – but seldom the work of an orthodox Minister at home. I buried no dead for that had to be left to the enemy. I preached no sermon – I passed Good Friday and Easter Sunday without being aware of them. But the last messages and the hurried talks at midnight, the ceaseless journeyings on behalf of the needs of the fighting men – these were part of my work. I walked until the bones of my feet felt as though they would go through my boots. I rode until my legs were raw and I was so tired I dared not sit on a horse. To stop was to sleep, anywhere, anyhow.

Source: Kenneth Lysons, *Robert Wilfrid Callin 1886–1951*, Gilpin Press, 1996, pp. 12–13.

who had enlisted by 1918, one tenth lost their lives in the war. Forty-three Primitive Methodist ministers served as chaplains to the forces, working under a United Chaplaincy Board with Baptist and Congregational colleagues[1] [74]. In recognition of the extraordinary strain and dangers of war, the minimum annual salaries of ministers were raised from £120 to £150 for superintendents, with a proportionate increase for their colleagues. The loss of nearly 1,000 male Sunday school teachers in the war prompted a much greater recruitment of women into this cause.[2]

Towards the end of the war the Wesleyans put out a joint invitation to the Primitives and United Methodists to form a united committee which might explore the way towards a truly united Methodism which would be a countrywide force for the evangelization of Britain. The two recipients of this Wesleyan proposal responded willingly. A Parliamentary Bill was enacted in 1928. Depending on each of the Connexions raising sufficient support, 1932 was to be the date of the fulfilment of the Bill.

In 1925 the Wesleyan Conference had decided that a 75 per cent vote in favour must be secured both in the Conference and Districts for any proposal on union. As this vote had not been achieved by 1927 the Wesleyan Conference appointed a committee of four to investigate. They presented a Policy of Three Stages, acceptance of the Enabling Bill in 1928, a final vote for Union in 1931, a Uniting Conference in 1932, and the first Conference of the United Church in 1933. The interim period was to be devoted to active preparation, and the 75 per cent formula was to be observed throughout. The Primitive Methodist and the United Methodist leaders accepted these Three Stages, as did subsequently their Conferences. The Representative Session of the Wesleyan Conference, and the Primitive Methodist and United Methodist Conferences all accepted the proposal for Methodist Union.[3]

The Union Committee meeting in the first week in June 1926 proposed the motion [75].

Methodism was in the toils of these great issues of unity but one has to ask whether the secular world

---

75. The united Committee reports that during the year it has prepared the Enabling Bill and New Model Deed, and now presents them to the three Conferences. It further presents the amended form of the Doctrinal and Sacramental clauses, and rejoices in the agreement which has been reached in regard to these important points. The committee, whilst giving due weight to the fact that there is still a minority in the three Churches whose votes have been cast against the present proposals, is of opinion that the time has come for the several Conferences to pronounce definitely upon the question. It therefore recommends that a resolution in favour of Union on the basis of the scheme as amended should be submitted to each of the three Conferences. The committee cherishes the hope that should the votes of the three Conferences be in favour of taking the necessary steps for the effecting of Union, many of those who at present take a different view will be ready to co-operate in carrying out the decision of the majority as voiced in each case by the supreme court of the Churches concerned.

Source: *Methodist Leader*, 10 June 1926.

---

took much notice of the debate. A sobering comment comes from a secular historian [76].

At the grass roots of Methodism, Union generated a multiplicity of knotty problems with regard to such issues as the boundaries of uniting circuits, chapel mergers and closures, ministerial appointments, and the disposal of surplus churches and manses. The working out of all this took many years to resolve, and no doubt in many localities memories of it linger on today. More intractable problems were those of sentiment, prejudice and deep-rooted local loyalties.

There was indeed much hard debate and anxiety, and each of the three Connexions was obliged to accept significant sacrifices in the negotiations. In the case of Primitive Methodism one such concession was the abandonment of a long-standing practice of a lay majority of 2:1 in their synods and conferences. The other two major Connexions had likewise to adjust elements within their constitutions. Nevertheless some long-cherished Primitive Methodist

76. It is not easy to assess the place of the churches in British life of the twenties. There was much talk of their failure to attract or to hold the loyalties of the younger generation. The rise of 'the Left' was, in some measure, indication of this. The new thought of the time – whether its prophet was Marx or Freud or Einstein – seemed to erode religious faith as the Churches had always preached it. Agnosticism was fashionable, and the leaders of literary taste went in for 'debunking' . . . The three main Methodist churches worked for union and gained it by 1932. But indifference remained a common attitude.

Source: David Thomson, *England in the Twentieth Century*, Penguin Edition, 1965, p. 119.

77. In 1929 the Methodist Church Union Act was passed by Parliament, and in 1932 the Methodist Church in Great Britain was formed. The Uniting Conference met in the Royal Albert Hall, London, on September 20th, 1932, in the presence of their Royal Highnesses, the Duke and Duchess of York, representing King George V and Queen Mary. The Deed of Union was read and signed. The Revd John Scott Lidgett, M.A., D.D., was elected the first President, Sir Robert W. Perks, Bart., Vice-President, and the Revd Robert Bond, Secretary of the Conference.

Source: Kenneth Garlick, *Methodist Registry*, London: Edsall, 1983, p. 41.

practices survived the complex debates of the Union negotiations. These included the appointment of lay men (and later lay women) into the office of Connexional Vice-President, and the acceptance of lay administration in the Sacrament of Holy Communion, though hedged with cautious restrictions. Throughout the long drawn-out discussions and negotiations Dr A. S. Peake (Primitive Methodism's superlative biblical scholar) proved to be a skilful and wise negotiator on behalf of Methodist Union and of Primitive Methodism's part in it. One much debated issue was whether the newly united Methodist Church should incorporate in its Annual Conference a session representing ministers alone. The Primitive Methodists had no such arrangement and there was a strong reluctance by them to accept it, but after extended debate the necessary 75 per cent majority in its favour was achieved [77].

The statistics of Primitive Methodism in 1932, and those of the other two Connexions, may be seen in the table below.

It is a pleasant and interesting coincidence that the last President and Vice-President of the Primitive Methodist Church, in the year of Methodist Union, were both reared in Northumberland. This remote region, as it undoubtedly seemed in the early years of the Connexion, proved to be one of the most prolific areas for the growth of Primitive Methodism and for the rearing of able leaders.

From his youth William Younger (1869–1956) experienced the hard conditions of life in mining communities, and, as many other miners did, he heard the call to preach and was accepted to train for the Primitive Methodist ministry at Hartley College. He was naturally an evangelist and a pastor too, and his 45 years as a minister were spent in only five circuits. He was a signatory to the Act of Union, and later Chairman of the Hull Synod. He was elected President of the Methodist Conference in 1934. He preached and lectured extensively not only within Britain but also in Europe and North America. Social themes including Temperance featured in his preaching and lecturing and he delivered the

	Ministers	Local Preachers	Members	Chapels	Sunday Schools
Wesley Methodists	2,510	18,785	517,551	8,152	6,952
Primitive Methodists	1,131	12,896	222,021	4,356	4,006
United Methodists	729	5,232	179,527	2,900	2,152

annual Hartley lecture in 1924. He was a keen Free-Churchman and advocated a union of the British Free Churches.

The Vice-President of the final Primitive Methodist Conference was Victor Murray, son of a working-class Northumbrian family who won a place to Magdalen College, Oxford, and went on to an academic career which led him to the Presidency of Cheshunt College, Cambridge. Murray was fond of declaring that the Primitive Methodists had much in common with the Congregationalists and should have united with them in 1932 rather than with the Wesleyans! His memories of Berwick Primitive Methodism were affectionate [78].

The final Conferences of the three contracting churches took place in the early summer of 1932 [79].

Despite the euphoria of the ceremonies most thoughtful Methodists knew that union was never

79. The Primitive Methodist Conference met for its final sittings in the town of Middlesbrough on June 13, and continued in session until June 22. The Revd William Younger was elected President, and Mr A. Victor Murray, M.A., B.Litt., Vice-President, with the General Secretary, the Revd Jacob Walton, in charge of the Agenda. The Conference unanimously nominated the Revd J. Scott Lidgett, M.A., D.D., as the President of the Uniting Conference, and Sir Robert W. Perks, Bart., as the first Vice-President. On June 22, it adjourned until Tuesday, September 20, to meet in London.

Source: R. Newman Wycherley, *The Pageantry of Methodist Union: Being a Pictorial Record of Events Leading up to and Consummating in the Historic Uniting Conference of 1932*, London: Epworth Press, 1936, p. 218.

78. Of all the buildings in Berwick I found our Primitive Methodist Chapel in College Place the most attractive. It was a haunt of ancient peace such as I had felt in Ravensdowne. It was shyly situated in a short quiet street just off Marygate and almost hidden by that part of the wall, so that you had to look for it if you wanted to find it. There was none of the vulgarity which these days insists on a central site in order to compete with the local cinema. The chapel stood in a little courtyard which also contained a house for the minister. Above the door of the house stood a bust of William Clowes, one of the founders of our denomination . . . It was quite unthinkable that anyone should give way to idle chatter as is all too common in many chapel congregations. The quietness of the place and the dignified dark wood of the pews all made for reverence and godly fear and had a great influence on a sensitive child.

Source: Albert Victor Murray, *A Northumbrian Methodist Childhood: Autobiographical Account of Family, Community and Chapel Life in Choppington and Berwick-upon-Tweed around the Turn of the 19th Century*, ed. Geoffrey E. Milburn, Northumberland County Library, 1992, pp. 56–7.

going to be easy. Even the most positively minded Primitive Methodists were aware that union involved a host of potential problems, and by no means were all positively minded. There were fears that the Primitive Methodist character and ethos would be threatened, and that beloved chapels would be threatened by closure. At the same time, most Primitive Methodists were realistic folk and knew that there was much logic in union, and that the merger made practical sense. So with a mixture of excitement, optimism and hard-headed realism on the one hand, and doubts, uncertainties and regrets on the other, the Primitive Methodists went forth into Union.

The ceremonies and acts of worship of the Union event itself had all the expected emotion and optimism. But realistic Primitive Methodists were aware that once the euphoria had calmed down they would have to face up to stern facts and look to the future. That future, however, was to be no longer contained within Primitive Methodism. For Methodists, a new age had begun.

The final Connexional Conferences to authorize this great step were held in 1932. The Primitive Conference met in Middlesbrough. The Uniting

80.   The Uniting Conference of 1932

After prolonged discussion and many vicissitudes, the three contracting Churches assembled in London on September 20, 1932, for the historic Uniting Conference. Sixty-six years had elapsed since the President of the Methodist New Connexion Conference first approached the Wesleyan Methodist Conference. Fifty-four years had gone since Sir Robert W. Perks had given his Notice of Motion in the Wesleyan Methodist Conference, and over forty years had gone since Hugh Price Hughes's fiery outburst at the Washington Ecumenical Conference.

The interval, though long, had been well used, for on September 20, 1932 the three Churches met, with a practically unanimous judgement. Since 1918 the investigations had been intensified; apparently insurmountable difficulties were gradually removed, while the fellowship of the meetings deepened in goodwill and fervour. The movement owes a lasting debt of gratitude to the three Secretaries, the Revs. E. Aldom French, Samuel Horton, and Henry Smith, for their statesmanlike skill, undaunted courage, and shining graciousness in woe as well as in weal.

Nearly fifteen hundred delegates and representatives, gathered from all parts of the world, soon realized their kinship in the family of Methodism and settled down happily and eagerly to write a vital page in the story of Protestant Christianity. Every member of the historic gatherings knew that a great cloud of witnesses encircled them. These highly-privileged Methodist ministers and laymen accepted the combined heritage of an illustrious past and prayed for wisdom and grace to enable them to transmit it enlarged and enriched to future Methodism.

Source: R. Newman Wycherley, *Pageantry of Methodist Union*, p. 224.

Conference began on 20 September at the Albert Hall, London [80]. Here the Deed of Union was signed in the presence of the Duke and Duchess of York, the future King George VI and his Queen. The votes cast by the Primitive Methodists in favour of this momentous step were 284 for and 4 against. The Duke of York read the King's message of interest and approval, and also spoke on his own account in appreciation of the 23,000 Methodist Churches, a quarter of a million members, and 53,000 local preachers [81].

A unique visual source for the Union of Methodism is a photograph taken at some point within the celebratory programme. About one metre in length it is a panorama of a vast crowd of Methodist folk, ministerial and lay, standing outside Westminster Abbey. The quality of the print is remarkable and there is no difficulty in recognizing faces, even on the far back rows. Grey hairs and bald heads

81. On Tuesday morning the 20th September 1932 the Uniting Conference opened with a devotional session at Wesley's Chapel. During this service the Revd William Younger, the President of the Primitive Methodist Conference, framed a 'brief address'. He got us and he got 'right there', as the Americans say, in his very first word: 'This is the first great hour of an historic week, and we are starting in an upper room.' There was no mistaking the truth and force of that note. It was a bold claim that our advantages were greater than those of the first upper room experience – greater by reason of the accumulated advantages of the centuries. 'What an upper room this is!' he exclaimed, reminding us that we are the custodians of spiritual treasures.

Mr Younger gave us an address – not a sermon – but nevertheless he had his points clearly arranged:– the upper room the place for realising new power and new intensity, and the only place of departure for every great spiritual enterprise: then he moved from the room to the Master. A beautiful picture could be imagined from the hints of Mr Younger. The picture of the Church as a home: the Master has the keys, 'only the keys which open doors of spiritual experience to every son of man open the doors of the Kingdom.' Then his description of a Chichester home with a mirror so arranged that the first thing seen within the house is a reflection of the Church. So he pleaded that the first thing to be seen in the Methodist home shall be Christ.

Source: 'Diary of the Conference: Impressions by "Mancunian"', *The Methodist Times and Leader*, 22 September 1932, p. 21.

tend to dominate the assembly which perhaps represents the sunset of divided Methodism rather more than the brave new world of the uniting church. But to the left of the crowd a busy London bus is a reminder of the bustling lay world to which the newly united Methodist Church is called to minister. To this Church the Primitive Methodists were bringing their resources, their chapels, their institutions, their publications and literature, and above all the loyalty and commitment of their members.

Seventy years later this legacy is largely forgotten, even by Methodists. The tendency among many Methodists since 1932 has been to diminish the unique character and achievements of the various former Methodist Connexions in order to stress the importance of unity and uniformity. Though understandable this would be a cause of regret if a part of the rich tapestry of Methodist development, in this case Primitive Methodism, were to be forgotten in the process.

This fine modern hymn can serve to express splendidly the authentic spirit and the character of Primitive Methodism which in changed circumstances still lives on today.

> The Church of Christ, in every age
>   Beset by change but Spirit-led,
> Must claim and test its heritage
>   And keep on rising from the dead.
>
> Across the world, across the street,
>   The victims of injustice cry
> For shelter and for bread to eat,
>   And never live until they die.

> Then let the servant Church arise,
>   A caring Church that longs to be
> A partner in Christ's sacrifice,
>   And clothed in Christ's humanity.
>
> For he alone, whose blood was shed,
>   Can cure the fever in our blood,
> And teach us how to share our bread
>   And feed the starving multitude.
>
> We have no mission but to serve
>   In full obedience to our Lord:
> To care for all, without reserve,
>   And spread his liberating Word.
>   *F. Pratt Green*
>   *Hymns and Psalms*, 804

If the churches of Britain are to be stirred to a genuine spirit of revival in our time the story of the Primitive Methodist Church in all its fulness stands as a model from which much inspiration and instruction can still be sought.

For discussion

1. Has the reading of this book changed your perceptions of Primitive Methodism?

2. Has Primitive Methodism any living legacy to hand on to Methodism today?

Appendix:

Englesea Brook Chapel and Museum of Primitive Methodism

Stephen G. Hatcher

The museum at Englesea Brook has been in the making since 1983. Englesea Brook as a place was on the first Primitive Methodist preaching plan of 1811, and was to be the chosen burial site of Hugh Bourne. The chapel at Englesea Brook dates from 1828, and served the local community for over a hundred and fifty years. Having become redundant by 1983, it seemed the ideal place to represent what Primitive Methodism had stood for.

The museum at Englesea Brook now contains artefacts that were the personal belongings of the founders: a walking stick and boot used by Hugh Bourne, and a lantern and stick belonging to William Clowes. It also contains very significant early exhibits including the chest-of-drawers cum pulpit that was used in Mr Smith's kitchen. Also can be seen here the printing press that was used by the Bourne brothers at Bemersley, and the organ of 1828, originating from Silsden, and the first such instrument to be used in Primitive Methodist worship.

The museum also brings to life the history of the movement with an audio-visual introduction, with magic-lantern slides, the voice of Thomas Russell from prison and other oral history recordings that can be listened to on a handset. Museum staff are always on duty to talk with visitors and help with interpretation. Souvenirs and second-hand books (including books about Methodism) are always available for sale.

However, the museum is part of a larger project, which also seeks to interpret the outward-looking dynamic spirit of the Primitive Methodists through engagement with contemporary society. Some of these activities are as follows:

1) Book sales have been held annually since 1984 based at Mow Cop, and are now also held at York and Poole. Many of the books come from Methodists

and through the sales go on to new readers (many of whom are preachers). The sale at Mow Cop has been a hive of activity with several hundred visitors flocking into the chapel. The activity has also raised funds for the development of Englesea Brook, with as much as £11,000 raised in one year.

2) Work with schools has been undertaken on a serious basis since 1998, with 100 visits to schools each year, and with 40 school groups annually visiting Englesea Brook. Local history, the Victorians, and themes of religious education make up a package that holds young people for up to four hours at a time. The use of costume and role-play of the Victorian working-class Sunday school makes this a memorable visit. The children also understand the part that faith played in the lives of the young Victorian workers who in many ways had so little to hope for, but who managed to find real hope through the rudimentary education provided by the Sunday school.

3) Englesea Brook has purchased a cottage to house the library and thereby enlarge research opportunities. The cottage is available at reasonable rates for those who want to come to study the movement, to visit the museum and explore the heritage of the area, or just have a good holiday break.

4) Englesea Brook is also working in co-operation with Mow Cop Chapel. The chapel, which was built in 1860 in the corner of the field where the first camp meeting was held, only has a small congregation and has fallen into disrepair. The partnership between Englesea Brook and Mow Cop will endeavour to renew the fabric and relate the work of the museum with communal and heritage activities.

5) Lectures and study days are held with the support of the Methodist Chapel Aid Association Limited.

Opening hours: April to November (inclusive) open every Thursday, Friday, Saturday and Bank Holiday Mondays 10.30 a.m.–5.00 p.m. Open every day during August apart from Monday.

Group visits should be pre-arranged, and can take place outside of normal opening hours.

Select Bibliography

The following list consists of standard works, articles and monographs that have been used in the writing of this book.

A fuller list of references can be found in the four volumes of Rupert Davies and Ernest Gordon Rupp (eds), *A History of the Methodist Church in Great Britain*, 4 vols, London: Epworth Press, 1965–88, and particularly in vol. 4. *The Primitive Methodist Magazine* (monthly), *Minutes of Conference* (annual) and John A. Vickers, *A Dictionary of Methodism in Britain and Ireland*, Peterborough: Epworth, 2000, have been invaluable sources throughout the book.

Antliff, William, *The Life of Hugh Bourne, founder of the Primitive Methodist Connexion*, rev. edn, London, 1892.

Arch, Joseph, *Joseph Arch: the story of his life*, 1898; *The Autobiography of Joseph Arch*, ed. John Gerard O'Leary, Fitzroy editions, London: Macgibbon & Kee, 1966.

Atkinson, John, *Life of Colin C. M'Kechnie*, London: Thomas Mitchell, 1898.

Barber, Benjamin Aquila, *A Methodist Pageant: A Souvenir of the Primitive Methodist Church*, London: Holborn Publishing House, 1932.

Bebbington, David W., *Evangelicalism in Modern Britain: A History from the 1730s to the 1980s*, Unwin Hyman, 1989; London: Routledge, 1993.

Beckworth, William Harold, *A Book of Remembrance, Being Records of Leeds Primitive Methodism Compiled during the Centenary Year, 1910*, London: W. A. Hammond, 1911.

Bourne, Hugh, *History of the Primitive Methodists, giving an account of their rise and progress, up to the year 1823*, Bemersley: printed for the author; copied and printed by W. Leary, 1994.

Bowran, John George, *The Life of Arthur Thomas Guttery D.D.*, Foreword by Rt Hon. David Lloyd George, London: Holborn Publishing House, 1922.

Bunting, Thomas Percival, and George Stringer Rowe, *The Life of Jabez Bunting, D.D., with notices of contemporary persons and events*, 2 vols, London: Longmans; T. Woolmer, 1887.

1851 Census of Great Britain: Report and Tables on Religious Worship: England and Wales, Parliamentary Paper lxxix, ed. Horace Mann, 1853.

Colls, Robert, *The Collier's Rant: Song and Culture in the Industrial Village*, London: Croom Helm, 1977.

Colls, Robert, *The Pitmen of the Northern Coalfield: Work, Culture, and Protest, 1790–1850*, Manchester: Manchester University Press, 1987.

Earnest Men: Sketches of Eminent Primitive Methodists. A Centenary of the Venerable Hugh Bourne, 1872.

Edwards, George, *From Crow-Scaring to Westminster: An Autobiography*, London: Labour Publishing Co., 1922.

Farndale, William Edward, *The Secret of Mow Cop*, Wesley Historical Society Lectures, no. 16, London: Epworth Press, 1950.

Flanagan, James, *Scenes from My Life, Both Grave and Gay . . .* , London: Hodder & Stoughton, 1907.

Garlick, Kenneth, *Methodist Registry*, London: Edsall, 1983.

Graham, E. Dorothy (comp.), *Chosen by God: A List of the Female Travelling Preachers of Early Primitive Methodism*, Wesley Historical Society Publishing, 1989.

Graham, E. Dorothy, *Three Colleges: Primitive Methodist Secondary Educational Venture*, 8th Chapel Aid Lecture, York: Englesea Brook Chapel, 1998.

Hall, Michael, *Ravers, Ranters and Respectable Schoolboys*, Bourne College, Quinton Local History Society and Quinton Methodist Chruch, 1981 and 2001.

Hatch, Nathan O., *The Democratization of American Christianity*, New Haven: Yale University Press, 1989.

Horn, Pamela, *Joseph Arch (1826–1919): The Farm Workers' Leader*, Kineton: The Roundwood Press, 1971.

Julian, John (ed.), *A Dictionary of Hymnology*, London: John Murray, 1892.

Kendall, Holliday Bickerstaffe, *The History of the Primitive Methodist Church*, 2 vols, London: Primitive Methodist Publishing House, *c.*1907.

Kendall, Holliday Bickerstaffe, *What Hath God Wrought*, London: Primitive Methodist Publishing House, *c.*1907.

Kendall, Holliday Bickerstaffe, *History of the Primitive Methodist Church*, rev. and enlarged edn, London: Joseph Johnson, 1919.

Kent, John, *Holding the Fort: Studies in Victorian Revivalism*, London: Epworth Press, 1978.

Lawson, John James (Baron Lawson), *Peter Lee*, London: Hodder & Stoughton, 1936; London: Epworth Press, 1949.

Lewis, Donald M. (ed.), *The Blackwell Dictionary of Evangelical Biography, 1730–1860 (Dictionary of Evangelical Biography)*, Oxford: Blackwell Reference, 1995.

Lysons, Kenneth, *A Little Primitive*, Buxton: Church in the Market Place, 2001.

Lysons, Kenneth, *Robert Wilfrid Callin 1886–1951*, Buxton: Church in the Market Place; Houghton-le-Spring: Gilpin Press, 1996.

Macpherson, James, *The Life and Labours of the Revd John Petty*, London: Conference Offices, 1870.

Milburn, Geoffrey E., *A School for the Prophets: The Origins of Ministerial Education in Primitive Methodism*, 1981; published to mark the centenary, 1881–1981, of Hartley Victoria College, Manchester.

Milburn, Geoffrey E., *Unique in Methodism: 100 years of Chapel Aid*, York: Englesea Brook Chapel and the Methodist Chapel Aid Association, 1990.

Moore, Robert, *Pitmen, Preachers and Politics: The Effects of Methodism in a Durham Mining Community*, London: Cambridge University Press, 1974.

Murray, Albert Victor, *A Northumbrian Methodist Childhood: Autobiographical Account of Family, Community and Chapel Life in Choppington and Berwick-upon-Tweed around the Turn of the 19th Century*, ed. Geoffrey E. Milburn, Northumberland County Library, 1992.

Oxberry, John, *Thomas Hepburn of Felling. What he did for miners*, Felling: Robt. Heslop, 1938 [1939].

Patterson, A. H., *From Hayloft to Temple: The Story of Primitive Methodism in Yarmouth*, London: Bryant, 1903.

Peake, Arthur Samuel, *The Life of Sir William Hartley*, London: Hodder & Stoughton, 1926.

Peake, Arthur Samuel, 'Tribute to Sir William Hartley', *Holborn Review*, January 1923.

Petty, John, *The History of the Primitive Methodist Connexion from its origin to the Conference of 1859*, London: Conference Offices, 1860.

Petty, John, *Memoir of the Life and Labours of the Revd Thomas Batty*, London: King, 1857.

Petty, John, *Systematic Theology: A Series of Lectures*, ed. C. C. M'Kechnie, London: George Lamb, Conference Offices, 1873.

Potter, William, *Thomas Jackson of Whitechapel: A Record of Fifty Years of Social and Evangelistic Enterprise*, Liverpool: C. Tinling & Co., 1929; London: Working Lads' Institute (W. Potter), 1929.

Probert, John Charles Cripps, *Primitive Methodism in Cornwall: A History and Sociology*, Redruth: the author, 1966.

Ritson, Joseph, *The Romance of Primitive Methodism*, 4th edn, London: Primitive Methodist Publishing House, 1909.

Robson, W. J. (ed.), *Silsden Primitive Methodism*, Silsden: Brigg Bros. Canal Works, 1910.

Roe, Henry, *Mission to Africa: being sketches of places, people, providence and personal experience*, London: F. H. Hurd, [1873].

Roe, Henry, *West African Scenes: being descriptions of Fernando Po, its climate, etc.*, London, 1874.

Rowntree, Joseph, and Arthur Sherwell, *The Temperance Problem and Social Reform*, London: Hodder & Stoughton, 1899.

Russell, R. W., *The Life of James Flanagan, Preacher, Evangelist, Author*, London: Holborn Publishing House, 1920.

Russell, Thomas, *Record of Events in Primitive Methodism*, London: William Lister; Leeds: John Parrott, 1869.

Sangster, William Edwin Robert, *Methodism Can Be Born Again*, London: Hodder & Stoughton, 1938.

Sellers, Ian, *The Hymnody of Primitive Methodism*, Chapel Aid Lecture 1998, York: Englesea Brook Chapel, 1993.

Short, Colin C., 'Robert Winfield and the Revivalists', *Proceedings of the Wesley Historical Society*, vol. 53, part 3, October 2001.

Telford, John, *The New Methodist Hymn-Book. Illustrated in History and Experience*, London: Epworth Press, 1934.

Thompson, J. Day, *The Church That Found Herself*, London: W. A. Hammond, Primitive Methodist Publishing House, 1912.

Tonks, W. C., *Victory in the Villages: History of Brinkworth Circuit*, Aberdare, 1907.

Travis, James, *Seventy-five Years: The Life and Work of James Travis as Seen by Himself, and as Judged by Others*, ed. John Day Thomson, London: W. A. Hammond, 1914.

Valenze, Deborah M., *Prophetic Sons and Daughters: Female Preaching and Popular Religion in Industrial England*, Princeton and Guildford: Princeton University Press, 1985.

Walford, John, *Memoirs of the Life and Labours of the Ven. Hugh Bourne 1772–1852*, Burslem, 1855–7.

Ward, William Reginald, *Faith and Faction*, London: Epworth Press, 1933.

Ward, William Reginald, *Religion and Society in England 1790–1850*, Fabric of British History, London: Batsford, 1972.

Watson, John Richard, *The English Hymn: A Critical and Historical Study*, Oxford: Clarendon Press, 1997.

Wearmouth, Robert Featherstone, *Methodism and the Working Class Movements of England, 1800–1850*, London: Epworth Press, 1937.

Werner, Julia Stewart, *The Primitive Methodist Connexion: Its Background and Early History*, Madison, WI: University of Wisconsin Press, 1984.

Wesley, John, *Letters*, ed. J. Telford, London: Epworth Press, 1931, vol. 5.

Wilkes, A., and J. Lovatt, *Mow Cop and the Camp Meeting Movement: Sketches of Primitive Methodism*, Leominster: Orphans Printing Press, 1942.

Wilkinson, John Thomas, *Arthur Samuel Peake: A Biography*, London: Epworth Press, 1971.

Wilkinson, John Thomas, *Hugh Bourne 1772–1852*, London: Epworth Press, 1952.

Wilkinson, John Thomas, *William Clowes 1780–1851*, London: Epworth Press, 1951.

Wilson, John, *Memories of a Labour Leader: The Autobiography of John Wilson J.P. M.P.*, 1910.

Woodcock, Henry, *Piety among the peasantry: being sketches of Primitive Methodism on the Yorkshire Wolds*, London: Joseph Toulson; Huddersfield: Primitive Methodist Book Depot, 1889.

Wycherley, R. Newman, *The Pageantry of Methodist Union: Being a Pictorial Record of Events Leading up to and Consummating in the Historic Uniting Conference of 1932*, London: Epworth Press, 1936.

Yarrow, William H., *History of Primitive Methodism in London*, London: Dickenson, 1876.

Notes

Introduction

1. John Hampson, *Memoirs of John Wesley: With a review of his life and writings, and a history of Methodism*, 3 vols, Sunderland, 1791, vol. 3, p. 10.
2. John Wesley, *Letters*, vol. 2, 1742–48, ed. J. Telford, London: Epworth Press, reprinted 1960, p. 292.
3. R. Alan Ker, 'The Origins of Primitive Wesleyan Methodism in Ireland', *Proceedings of the Wesley Historical Society*, xliii, part 4, May 1982, pp. 77–85.
4. Thomas Percival Bunting and George Stringer Rowe, *The Life of Jabez Bunting, D.D., with notices of contemporary persons and events*, London: Longmans; T. Woolmer, 1887, p. 252.

1. Origins

1. See William Reginald Ward, *Religion and Society in England 1790–1850*, Fabric of British History, London: Batsford, 1972; Julia Stewart Werner, *The Primitive Methodist Connexion: Its Background and Early History*, Madison, WI: University of Wisconsin Press, 1984; Holliday Bickerstaffe Kendall, *The History of the Primitive Methodist Church*, 2 vols, London: Primitive Methodist Publishing House, c.1907, vol. 1, pp. 7–156.
2. John Thomas Wilkinson, *Hugh Bourne 1772–1852*, London: Epworth Press, 1952, pp. 24–7.
3. Kendall, *History of the Primitive Methodist Church*, vol. 1, p. 12.
4. *Methodist Magazine* (Wesleyan), 1807, p. 452.
5. Holliday Bickerstaffe Kendall, *What Hath God Wrought*, London: Primitive Methodist Publishing House, c.1907, pp. 15–16.
6. On Dow, see Nathan O. Hatch, *The Democratization of American Christianity*, New Haven: Yale University Press, 1989, *passim*.
7. John Petty, *The History of the Primitive Methodist Connexion from its origin to the Conference of 1859*, London: Conference Offices, 1860, pp. 12–14.
8. Petty, *History of the Primitive Methodist Connexion*, p. 9.

2. Early growth

1. John Wesley, *Letters*, ed. J. Telford, London: Epworth Press, 1931, vol. 5, p. 257.
2. Hugh Bourne, *History of the Primitive Methodists, giving an account of their rise and progress, up to the year 1823*, Bemersley: printed for the author; copied and printed by W. Leary, 1994, p. 39.
3. Bourne, *History of the Primitive Methodists*, p. 57.
4. Donald M. Lewis (ed.), *The Blackwell Dictionary of Evangelical Biography, 1730–1860* (*Dictionary of Evangelical Biography*), Oxford: Blackwell Reference, 1995: entry under 'Crawfoot'.
5. Kendall, *What Hath God Wrought*, p. 15.
6. Kendall, *History of the Primitive Methodist Church*, vol. 1, pp. 559 and 113.
7. John Parrott, *A Digest of the History, Polity and Doctrines of the Primitive Methodists*, 2nd edn enlarged, London: R. Davies, 1864, pp. 78–80.
8. Stephen Hatcher, 'Sacrament of the Lord's Supper in Early Primitive Methodism', *Proceedings of the Wesley Historical Society*, May 1990, pp. 229–30.
9. E. Dorothy Graham (comp.), *Chosen by God: A List of the Female Travelling Preachers of Early Primitive Methodism*, Wesley Historical Society Publishing, 1989.
10. Kendall, *What Hath God Wrought*, p. 23.
11. William Edwin Robert Sangster, *Methodism Can Be Born Again*, London: Hodder & Stoughton, 1938, p. 12.

12. Petty, *History of the Primitive Methodist Connexion*, p. 73.
13. Kendall, *History of the Primitive Methodist Church*, vol. 1, pp. 257–8.
14. Kendall, *History of the Primitive Methodist Church*, vol. 1, p. 258.
15. Stephen Hatcher, 'The Significance of William Clowes', *Wesley Historical Society, North East Bulletin*, 34, September 1980, pp. 15–17.
16. 'The Countess of Carlisle: One of our helpers, By a Personal Friend', *Primitive Methodist Magazine*, 1896, pp. 357–9.

3. A mid-century survey

1. Appendix, *Primitive Methodist Consolidated Minutes*, London: Thomas Holliday, Conference Offices and Book Room, 1849.
2. William Reginald Ward, 'The Religion of the People and the Problem of Control 1790–1830', *Faith and Faction*, London: Epworth Press, 1993, pp. 264–84; first published in *Studies in Church History*, 8, 1971, pp. 237–57.
3. *1851 Census of Great Britain: Report and Tables on Religious Worship: England and Wales*, Parliamentary Paper lxxix, ed. Horace Mann, 1853, p. clxi.
4. John Hunt, *Wesley and Wesleyanism: Three Lectures*, London; Sunderland, 1858, p. 50.
5. Petty, *History of the Primitive Methodist Connexion*, p. 386.
6. *Primitive Methodist Magazine*, 1837, p. 352.
7. *Primitive Methodist Magazine*, 1844, pp. 156–7.
8. *Primitive Methodist Magazine*, 1841, pp. 252–4.
9. *Primitive Methodist Magazine*, 1872, pp. 1–11.
10. Quoted in John Thomas Wilkinson, *William Clowes 1780–1851*, London: Epworth Press, 1951, pp. 76–7.

4. Becoming a church

1. The fullest account is James Macpherson, *The Life and Labours of the Revd John Petty*, London: Conference Offices, 1870. See also the piece on Petty (especially the references) by Geoffrey E. Milburn, *From Mow Cop to Peake 1807–1932: Essays to Commemorate the 175th Anniversary of the Beginnings of Primitive Methodism*, Occasional Paper 4, Yorkshire Branch, Wesley Historical Society, 1982.
2. Macpherson, *Life and Labours of the Revd John Petty*, p. 201.
3. Petty, *History of the Primitive Methodist Connexion*, p. 441.
4. Petty, *History of the Primitive Methodist Connexion*, p. 445.
5. Petty, *History of the Primitive Methodist Connexion*, pp. 446–7.
6. See below in this chapter.
7. For accounts of Primitive Methodist overseas missions in the colonies and other foreign parts, see Kendall, *History of the Primitive Methodist Church*, vol. 2, bk 3, chs 5 and 7. A briefer account can be found in Benjamin Aquila Barber, *A Methodist Pageant: A Souvenir of the Primitive Methodist Church*, London: Holborn Publishing House, 1932, pp. 167–96. Henry Roe himself wrote two books, *West African Scenes: being descriptions of Fernando Po, its climate, etc.*, London, 1874, and *Mission to Africa: being sketches of places, people, providence and personal experience*, London: F. H. Hurd, [1873], describing Primitive Methodist missionary work in that continent. A useful chapter in James Travis, *Seventy-five Years: The Life and Work of James Travis as Seen by Himself, and as Judged by Others*, ed. John Day Thompson, London: W. A. Hammond, 1914, covers the years from 1889 to 1894, when Travis held the post of Primitive Methodist Missionary Secretary. And there are some interesting pages on the earliest colonial mission in Petty, *History of the Primitive Methodist Connexion*, pp. 414–23.
8. *Earnest Men: Sketches of Eminent Primitive Methodists. A Centenary of the Venerable Hugh Bourne*, 1872, p. 241.
9. Joseph Ritson, *The Romance of Primitive Methodism*, 4th edn, London: Edwin Dalton; Primitive Methodist Publishing House, 1909, p. 199.
10. Travis, *Seventy-five Years*, pp. 117–18.
11. *Primitive Methodist Minutes*, 1928, p. 260.
12. *Primitive Methodist Minutes*, 1925, p. 7.
13. E. Dorothy Graham, *Three Colleges: Primitive Methodist Secondary Educational Venture*, 8th Chapel Aid Lecture, York: Englesea Brook Chapel, 1998, p. 40.
14. Milburn, 'John Petty 1807–1868', *From Mow Cop to Peake*.
15. Graham, *Three Colleges*, pp. 6–49.
16. Geoffrey E. Milburn, *A School for the Prophets: The Origins of Ministerial Education in Primitive Meth-*

odism, 1981; published to mark the centenary, 1881–1981, of Hartley Victoria College, Manchester.

17. For these developments, see Milburn, *School for the Prophets*.

5. *Tensions and progress*

1. The principal evidence for this chapter is to be found in Geoffrey Milburn, 'Tensions in Primitive Methodism in the Eighteen-seventies', *Proceedings of the Wesley Historical Society*, xl, 4, February 1976, pp. 93–101, and 5, June 1976, pp. 135–43.

2. See John Kent, *Holding the Fort: Studies in Victorian Revivalism*, London: Epworth Press, 1978, a critical study of the influence upon English religion of American revivalists, from Lorenzo Dow to Dwight L. Moody and Ira D. Sankey, upon British religion. For a study of revival and revivalists in the north east during the mid-Victorian period, see Geoffrey E. Milburn, 'Revival and Revivalists in North-Eastern Mehodism in the Mid-Victorian Period', *Bulletin 20 of the North-East Branch of the Wesley Historical Society*, October 1973, pp. 12–16. See also David W. Bebbington, *Evangelicalism in Modern Britain: A History from the 1730s to the 1980s*, Unwin Hyman, 1989; London: Routledge, 1993, for the broader setting of revivalism.

3. *Sunderland Daily Echo*, 17 and 21 January 1876 and 16 February 1877.

4. Kendall, *History of the Primitive Methodist Church*, vol. 2, p. 205.

5. Kendall, *History of the Primitive Methodist Church*, vol. 2, pp. 455–6.

6. Kendall, *History of the Primitive Methodist Church*, vol. 2, pp. 458–63; *Primitive Methodist Magazine*, 1898, pp. 27–32 and 186–9.

7. *Primitive Methodist Magazine*, 1907, pp. 46–50.

8. *Primitive Methodist Magazine*, 1898, pp. 936–43.

9. T. S. Widdowson, 'Papers on Popular Antiquities: The Ruthwell Cross', *Primitive Methodist Magazine*, 1896, p. 57–60.

10. Kendall, *History of the Primitive Methodist Church*, vol. 2, pp. 530–1.

11. *Primitive Methodist Magazine*, 1931, p. 143.

6. *Social influence*

1. On Hepburn, see: *Primitive Methodist Magazine*, 1865, pp. 546–7; *Primitive Methodist Quarterly Review*, 1882, pp. 385–97; E. Norma Graham, 'Thomas Hepburn', *Wesley Historical Society North East Bulletin*, 16, pp. 9–14; Geoffrey E. Milburn, 'A Pioneer Miner', *Wesley Historical Society North East Bulletin*, 26, pp. 4–8; John Oxberry, *Thomas Hepburn of Felling. What he did for miners*, Felling: Robt. Heslop, 1938 [1939]; Robert Colls, *The Pitmen of the Northern Coalfield: Work, Culture, and Protest, 1790–1850*, Manchester: Manchester University Press, 1987.

2. Robert Featherstone Wearmouth, *Methodism and the Working Class Movements of England, 1800–1850*, London: Epworth Press, 1937, pp. 228–9.

3. Pamela Horn, *Joseph Arch (1826–1919): The Farm Workers' Leader*, Kineton: The Roundwood Press, 1971.

4. Robert Featherstone Wearmouth, *Methodism and the Struggle of the Working Classes, 1850–1900*, Leicester: Edgar Backus, 1954.

5. Edwin Thompson, 'Pioneers of Conciliation: Thomas Burt and John Wilson', *Wesley Historical Society North East Bulletin*, 47, March 1987, pp. 9–19; Barbara Anderson, 'The Life and Work of John Wilson', *Wesley Historical Society North East Bulletin*, 26, September 1976; S. Horton, 'An Interview with Mr John Wilson, M.P.', *Primitive Methodist Magazine*, 1896, pp. 687–91; John Wilson, *Memories of a Labour Leader: The Autobiography of John Wilson J.P. M.P.*, 1910. See also Thomas Burt, 'Methodism and the Northern Miners', *Primitive Methodist Quarterly Review*, 1882. On Peter Lee, see John James Lawson (Baron Lawson), *Peter Lee*, London: Hodder & Stoughton, 1936; London: Epworth Press, 1949.

6. Thomas Burt, 'Methodism and the Northern Miners', *Primitive Methodist Quarterly Review*, 1882, pp. 385–97.

7. *Wesley Historical Society North East Bulletin*, 34, p 17.

8. Robert Moore, *Pitmen, Preachers and Politics: The Effects of Methodism in a Durham Mining Community*, London: Cambridge University Press, 1974.

9. George Shaw, 'Men and Women I have known: Mr.

John Sissons, of Hull', *Primitive Methodist Magazine*, 1896, pp. 374–80 and 513–16.

10. Geoffrey E. Milburn, 'Piety, Profit and Paternalism: Methodists in Business in the North East of England', *Proceedings of the Wesley Historical Society*, December 1983, pp. 45–69.

11. John A. Vickers, *A Dictionary of Methodism in Britain and Ireland*, Peterborough: Epworth, 2000, p. 34.

12. Vickers, *Dictionary of Methodism in Britain and Ireland*, pp. 320 and 299.

13. Wilkinson, *Hugh Bourne*, p. 149.

14. Wilkinson, *Hugh Bourne*, pp. 156, 158 and 174.

15. Arthur Samuel Peake, *The Life of Sir William Hartley*, London: Hodder & Stoughton, 1926, ch. 12.

16. Joseph Rowntree and Arthur Sherwell, *The Temperance Problem and Social Reform*, London: Hodder & Stoughton, 1899, p. xiii.

17. Clive Field, 'The Devil in Solution: How Temperate Were the Methodists?' *Epworth Review*, July 2000, pp. 78–93.

18. William Potter, *Thomas Jackson of Whitechapel: A Record of Fifty Years of Social and Evangelistic Enterprise*, Liverpool: C. Tinling & Co., 1929; London: Working Lads' Institute (W. Potter), 1929, p. 159.

19. R. W. Russell, *The Life of James Flanagan, Preacher, Evangelist, Author*, London: Holborn Publishing House, 1920. See also S. Horton, 'An Interview with the Rev. James Flanagan', *Primitive Methodist Magazine*, 1898, pp. 762–9; Flanagan wrote an autobiography, *Scenes from My Life, Both Grave and Gay . . .* , London: Hodder & Stoughton, 1907.

7. *Primitive Methodist hymnody*

1. Hugh Bourne, Preface, *Large Hymn Book, for the use of the Primitive Methodists*, Bemersley: Office of the Primitive Methodist Connexion, 1829, pp. 2–6.

2. W. M. Patterson, *Northern Primitive Methodism*, London: E. Dalton, 1909, p. 125.

3. On Sanders, see A. Wilkes and J. Lovatt, *Mow Cop and the Camp Meeting Movement: Sketches of Primitive Methodism*, Leominster: Orphans Printing Press, 1942, pp. 82–7.

4. John Telford, the Wesleyan scholar, sadly revealed an unfortunate ignorance of Sanders in his entry on 'Hark the Gospel News', *The New Methodist Hymn-Book. Illustrated in History and Experience*, London:

Epworth Press, 1934, p. 171. What he writes about Sanders is completely incorrect apart from his date of birth. It was an unfortunate lapse in a book representing the union of Methodism. In John Richard Watson's major study, *The English Hymn: A Critical and Historical Study*, Oxford: Clarendon Press, 1997, there is no reference whatsoever to Primitive Methodist hymnody.

5. Kendall, *History of the Primitive Methodist Church*, vol. 2, pp. 257–8.

6. Julian, John (ed.), *A Dictionary of Hymnology*, London: John Murray, 1892, p. 730.

7. Petty, *History of the Primitive Methodist Connexion*, p. 545.

8. For a vivid personal response to the subject matter of this chapter, see the late Ian Sellers's, *The Hymnody of Primitive Methodism*, Chapel Aid Lecture 1993, York: Englesea Brook Chapel, 1993.

8. *The Hartley era*

1. Peake, *Life of Sir William Hartley*.

2. Arthur Samuel Peake, 'Tribute to Sir William Hartley', *Holborn Review*, January 1923.

3. Peake, 'Tribute to Sir William Hartley', pp. 1 and 6.

9. *The Primitive Methodist Centenary*

1. Jane Johnson and A. Greutzner (comps), *The Dictionary of British Artists, 1880–1940: An Antique Collectors' Club Research Project, Listing 41,000 Artists*, Woodbridge: Antique Collectors' Club, 1976, p. 503; Jane Johnson (comp.), *Works Exhibited at the Royal Society of British Artists, 1824–1893: An Antique Collectors' Club Research Project*, Woodbridge: Antique Collectors' Club, 1975, p. 462.

2. Barber, *Methodist Pageant*, has a monochrome print of the picture at the opening of the book.

3. Kendall, *History of the Primitive Methodist Church*, 1889, p. 36.

4. J. D. Thompson, *The Church That Found Herself*, p. 67.

10. *Towards Union*

1. Holliday Bickerstaffe Kendall, *History of the Primitive Methodist Church*, rev. and enlarged edn, London: Joseph Johnson, 1919, p. 169.

2. *Primitive Methodist Minutes*, 1918, p. 3–4; Kendall, *History of the Primitive Methodist Church*, 1919, pp. 168–70.

3. Kenneth Garlick, *Methodist Registry*, London: Edsall, 1983, p. 41.

Index